THE REP
Birmingham Repertory Theatre

Birmingham Repertory Theatre Company presents

First
Person
Shooter

by Paul Jenkins

T0347064

First performed at The Door, Birmingham Repertory Theatre
on 30 September 2010

FIRST PERSON SHOOTER

by **Paul Jenkins**

MAGGIE	Freya Copeland
ADE	Bradley Hall
CAPTAIN JONES / NUGGET	David Hounslow
TOM	Ben Jones

Director	Robert Shaw Cameron
Designer	Jess Curtis
AV Designer	Barret Hodgson
Lighting Designer	Richard G Jones
Sound Designer	Dan Hoole
Casting Director	Sarah Hughes
Dramaturg	Caroline Jester

Stage Manager	Paul Southern
Deputy Stage Manager	Neil Wilder

Cast

Freya Copeland (MAGGIE)
Freya trained at Webber Douglas Academy of Dramatic Art. Theatre work includes: *The Maintenance Man* (UK tour); *A View from the Bridge* (Bolton Octagon; Evening News Best Actress Nominee); *Romeo and Juliet* (Stafford Shakespeare Festival); *Bad Girls – The Musical* (original workshop, Old Vic); *Brassed Off* (National Theatre/Sheffield Crucible); *Marat Sade*, *Guys and Dolls*, *Snakehips* (National Theatre); *Passion* (West End); *The Three Musketeers* (Welsh Centre); *Twelfth Night* (Clivedon Open Air Festival); *Brideshead Revisited* (tour); *Give a Girl a Break* (Actors Centre). Pantomimes include: *Babes in the Wood*, *Jack and the Beanstalk*, *Cinderella* (Gatehouse Theatre, Stafford); *Hansel and Gretel* (Secombe Theatre, Surrey); *Mother Goose* (Churchill Theatre, Bromley). Television work includes: *Emmerdale*, *The Bill*, *Doctors*, *The Royal*, *Casualty*, *Law and Order UK*. Film work includes: *The Resurrectionist*. Recordings include: *Passion – Concert Performance*.

Bradley Hall (ADE)
Theatre work includes: *He* (Firehouse Creative Productions). Television and film work includes: *The Bill*, *Rite*, *Where the Monsters Go*, *Mercy*, *Spider*.

David Hounslow (CAPTAIN JONES / NUGGET)
David trained at Manchester Polytechnic School of Theatre. Theatre work includes: *The Snowman* (Leicester Haymarket); *Othello*, *Henry V*, *Coriolanus*, *The Wives' Excuse*, *Zenobia* (RSC); *Bent*, *Fuente Ovejuna* (National Theatre); *Treasure Island* (Farnham Redgrave); *Billy Budd* (Sheffield Crucible); *Our Boys* (Cockpit Theatre); *All of You Mine* (Bush Theatre); *Perpetua*, *My Night with Reg*, *Dealer's Choice* (Birmingham Repertory Theatre); *Alcestis* (Northern Broadsides); *Tales from Hollywood*, *Privates On Parade* (Donmar Warehouse); *Holes in the Skin* (Chichester Festival Theatre); *The Rise and Fall of Little Voice* (Manchester Royal Exchange); *A Night at the Dogs* (Soho Theatre); *Tamburlaine* (Bristol Old Vic); *Billy Liar* (Liverpool Playhouse); *Warm* (Theatre503). Television work includes: *The Unknown Soldier*, *True Blues*, *Othello*, *Children of the North*, *Gone to the Dogs*, *The Bill*, *Resnick*, *True Crimes*, *Minder*, *Bad Company*, *Under the Hammer*, *Anna Lee*, *Soldier Soldier*, *Deadly Crack*, *The Cinder Path*, *Chandler and Co.*, *Six Sides of Coogan*, *Crime and Punishment*, *Turning World*, *Is It Legal?*, *Peak Practice*, *A Wing and a Prayer*, *Dangerfield*, *Playing the Field*, *Bugs*, *Within Living Memory*, *Casualty*, *EastEnders*, *City Central*, Spencer in *Bomber*, *Always*

and Everyone, Other People's Children, Silent Witness, North Square, Heartbeat, London's Burning, Margery and Gladys, Ultimate Force, Crisis Command. He played series regular Jim Allbright in the critically acclaimed *Blackpool* and has recently appeared in *Holby City, The Brief, Robin Hood, Jekyll, Dalziel and Pascoe, Is This Love?, Little Miss Jocelyn, MI High, Dead Set, Bonekickers, Waking the Dead, Spooks IX, London Kills Me, Captives, Feverpitch.* Film work includes: *The Man Who Knew Too Little, I Want You, Tabloid, The Flying Scotsman.* Radio work includes: *Cabs* (Piccadilly Radio, Manchester); *Alcestis, S* (both for BBC Radio).

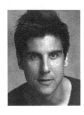

Ben Jones (TOM)

Ben has spent several years touring new writing with plays such as Uzmah Hameed's *Taj* and *A Dark River* (national tour and Riverside Studios), and Judith Adams's *The Bone Room* (Young Vic). He also played both Athos and Richelieu in the Common Players' open-air UK tour of *The Three Musketeers.* He recently played the part of Adam in Alan Ayckbourn's *Time of My Life* at the Royal and Derngate Theatre in Northampton, and Piers in *The Pretender Agenda* in London's West End. Ben is best known for his recent TV credits: as regular Dr Greg Robinson in the BBC drama *Doctors* (2003–2007), and can also be seen in *Spooks, Holby City, Echo Beach, Moving Wallpaper* (BBC); *Longitude* (Channel 4); and *Keen Eddie* (Paramount/Fox). Ben has received nominations for Best Actor in the coveted Rose D'Or and Royal Television Society Awards. He was also nominated several times for 'Sexiest Male' in the British Soap Awards, which he never won. He doesn't like to talk about it.

Creative Team

Paul Jenkins (Writer)
Theatre work includes: *Underwater Love* (The Factory/Hampstead Theatre); *Natural Selection* (Munich State Theatre and Theatre503, London); *1984* (The Factory, Round 2); and *Island Hopping* (Belarus Free Theatre). Television and film work includes: *Casualty*, *EastEnders* and the Russian feature *Plus One* (English dialogue).

Robert Shaw Cameron (Director)
Robert is Resident Associate Director at The REP; he trained at Webber Douglas Academy of Dramatic Art and the University of Birmingham. He has worked as both director and actor in theatre and television. As Director: *Just So*, *Grass Routes: Cuttings* (Birmingham Repertory Theatre); *White Open Spaces* (Soho Theatre/UK tour/National Theatre of Sweden); *A Florentine Tragedy* (Florence); *1.60.3600* (Regent Park Studio/Young Vic); *Love at First* (Edinburgh); *Road*, *Guys and Dolls*, *Blood Wedding*, *Queen Coal*, *The Crucible* (University of Cumbria); *The Ribbon Cage* (RADA). As Assistant Director: *Arthur & George*, *Respect* (Birmingham Repertory Theatre); *The Taming of the Shrew*, *A Midsummer Night's Dream*, *The Boyfriend* (Regent's Park); *The Castle Spectre*. As an actor, theatre work includes: *Smoke*, *As You Like It* (New Vic); *Dracula*, *Precious Bane*, *Death of a Salesman*, *A Christmas Carol* (UK tours). Television and film work includes: *The Bill*, *The Wild Life*, *Shane*, *Where the Heart Is*, *The Basil Brush Show*, *EastEnders*, *Holby City*, *Heartbeat*, *Keen Eddie* and the feature film *Ibsen's Ghosts*.

Jess Curtis (Designer)
Jess trained at the Motley Theatre Design Course. Recent theatre work includes: *Another Door Closed* (Peter Hall Company); *Mary Stuart* (Hipp, Malmo Stadsteatre); *The Little Prince*, *Local Boy* (Hampstead Theatre); *Endgame* (Liverpool Everyman); *Rhapsody* (for the Royal Ballet Frederick Ashton Anniversary Celebrations, Royal Opera House, revived February 2007); *Fantasy* (Royal Ballet, Lindbury Studio); *Dangerous Corner* (West Yorkshire Playhouse/West End); *Frankenstein* (Frantic Assembly/Royal Theatre, Northampton); *My Zinc Bed*, *Follies*, *The Glass Cage* (Royal Theatre, Northampton); *She Stoops to Conquer*, *Burial at Thebes* (Nottingham Playhouse/Barbican PIT/US tour); *The Wizard of Oz* (West Yorkshire Playhouse); *Cinderella* (Oxford Playhouse); *Twelfth Night* (Open Air Theatre Regent's Park); *Rookery Nook* (Oxford Stage Company); *Black Crows* (Clean Break at the Arcola and tour); *The Daughter-in-Law*, *The Beauty Queen of Leenane* (Watford Palace Theatre). Opera work includes: *Stiffelio*, *Lucia de Lammermoor* (Holland Park Opera); *Macbeth*, *Bastien und Bastienne* (Nordjyllands Opera Denmark); *Così fan tutte* (Opera Ystad, Sweden); *A Rake's Progress*, *Don Giovanni* (Royal Academy of Music and Drama).

Barret Hodgson (AV Designer)
Barret is a new-media artist, film-maker and digital alchemist, based in Nottingham. His company Vent Media specialises in creating digital video, motion graphics and live interactive media for theatre and the live arts. Recent shows include: *Arthur & George* (Birmingham Repertory Theatre); *Smile* and *Empty Bed Blues* by Stephen Lowe; *Garage Band* by Andy Barrett and *Flat Stanley*. Barret studied Fine Arts BA (Hons) at the

Newcastle-upon-Tyne University and, more recently, on the Collaborative Arts Practice MA at Trent University, Nottingham. More information can be found on his website, www.ventmedia.co.uk

Richard G Jones (Lighting Designer)

Richard lit the actor-musician Broadway production of *Sweeney Todd* at the Eugene O'Neill Theater in New York, for which he was nominated for an Outer Critics Circle Award and won a Drama Desk Award for Outstanding Lighting Design. For Birmingham Repertory Theatre, work includes: *Blues in the Night*, *Ridin' the Number 8*, and a co-production with Graeae Theatre Company of *Whiter than Snow*. West End work includes: *Sunset Boulevard*, *Mack and Mabel*, *Sweeney Todd*, *Horrid Henry – Live and Horrid!*, *Steptoe and Son*, *When Pigs Fly*, *Female Parts*. Other lighting designs include: *The Homecoming*, *Death of a Salesman*, *A Taste of Honey*, *A Man for all Seasons* (York Theatre Royal); *The Man Who*, *Chicken Soup with Barley*, *The White Album* (Nottingham Playhouse); *Spongebob Squarepants: The Sponge that Could Fly!* (UK and South African tours); *Ich war noch niemals in New York* (Operettanhaus in Hamburg, Germany). Richard has recently lit: *The Railway Children* at the old Eurostar terminal at Waterloo Station; *The Hot Mikado*, *Copacabana* (Watermill Theatre, Newbury); *Oliver Twist*, *The Hired Man* (Bolton Octagon); *A Pair of Pinters* (Derby Live); *Canterbury Tales* (Northern Broadsides); *City of Angels* (Bridewell Theatre, London); *Behud* (Soho Theatre). Richard is currently working on designs for *Amy's View* (Nottingham Playhouse); *Jack and the Beanstalk* (York Theatre Royal); and *Celebrating Christmas* for the Salvation Army at the Royal Albert Hall.

Sarah Hughes (Casting Director)

Sarah was Alan Ayckbourn's Casting Director for seventeen years before he stepped down as Artistic Director of the Stephen Joseph Theatre in April 2009. She has worked for the last eight years as a freelance casting director for the BBC, where shows include *Pulling*, *Love Soup*, *Rock and Chips*, and the forthcoming second series of *The Old Guys*. Her freelance theatre casting includes shows for West Yorkshire Playhouse, Theatre Royal Northampton and the Mill at Sonning, and she recently cast *Othello* and *Frankenstein* for Frantic Assembly. She is happily continuing her working relationship with the SJT, and also works as a freelance lecturer. Sarah Hughes is a member of the Casting Directors Guild.

Caroline Jester (Dramaturg)

Caroline is Dramaturg at Birmingham Repertory Theatre and has taught on the MPhil in Playwriting at Birmingham University and various undergraduate programmes. She is the co-author of *Playwriting Across the Curriculum*, which will be published by Routledge in June 2011, and has worked as a freelance dramaturg, director and workshop leader.

With thanks to Emily Holt, Melissa Morgan, Alan Dickenson, Anna Himali – Howard and Tim Hewlett.

THE REP

Birmingham Repertory Theatre

Birmingham Repertory Theatre is one of Britain's leading national producing theatre companies. From its base in Birmingham, The REP produces over twenty new productions each year.

Artistic Director Rachel Kavanaugh's season of work for Autumn and Winter 2010 includes an adaptation by Tom Stoppard of Chekhov's *The Cherry Orchard* and a spellbinding musical adaptation of *The Secret Garden* at Christmas.

The commissioning and production of new work lies at the core of The REP's programme. The Door was established twelve years ago as a theatre dedicated to the production and presentation of new writing. In this time, it has given world premieres to new plays from a new generation of British playwrights. The Door aims to provide a distinct alternative to the work seen in the Main House: a space where new voices and contemporary stories could be heard, that sought to create new audiences for the work of the company, in this city and beyond. The Door has been a place to explore new ideas and different approaches to making theatre, to develop new plays and support emerging companies and artists.

Developing new and particularly younger audiences is also at the heart of The REP's work. The theatre's Learning and Participation department engages with over 10,000 young people each year through its various initiatives, including The Young REP, REP's Children, Grass Routes writing programme, and the Transmissions young writers' programme. Grass Routes is for young artists aged 18–30 wishing to explore different ways of telling stories onstage, from playwriting to spoken word to grime theatre. Transmissions has worked with hundreds of writers aged 12–25 across the region, and the theatre's Playwriting Officer delivers programmes in schools to help establish playwriting in the National Curriculum.

The REP's productions regularly transfer to London and tour nationally and internationally. Tours during 2009 included a new staging of Philip Pullman's *His Dark Materials*, Dennis Kelly's *Orphans*, Simon Stephens' *Pornography*, Charlie Dark's *Have Box Will Travel*, *Looking for Yogurt*, a new play for young children which played at theatres in the UK, Japan and Korea, and *These Four Streets*, a multi-authored play about the 2005 Lozells disturbances.

In 2009 our production of *The Snowman* made its international debut at the Seoul Opera House, Korea, before returning to the UK for a 12th Christmas season at London's Peacock Theatre and a January run at The REP. Plans are underway for the show to travel further afield during 2010.

2010–2013 will be a significant period of development in the history of Birmingham Repertory Theatre as it integrates with the new £193 million Library of Birmingham, which will be built adjacent to the theatre. This development opportunity will allow the theatre to make many improvements to its current building as well as sharing a new 300-seat flexible studio theatre with the Library of Birmingham. The period will bring an exciting time artistically as audiences will be able to enjoy and experience an imaginative programme of REP productions in other theatres and non-theatrical spaces across Birmingham.

The Library of Birmingham project has also enabled The REP to rethink its new-writing policy, and with the intended third space, The Door will no longer be the only venue for the development and production of new work. This brings with it more opportunities to encourage new writing and to consolidate the new work that already happens outside of The Door. The diversity of this new-writing work includes: early years' work, new plays for The Young REP – the theatre's resident youth theatre, adaptations, responding to specific briefs, community plays, writer/performer collaborative writing, site-specific work and incorporating digital technology into the development and production of work. In addition to the commissioning of this work, The REP runs a writers' attachment programme aimed at enabling playwrights to experiment with new forms. In collaboration with the BME Theatre Initiative, supported by Arts Council, England (West Midlands), The REP aims to constantly explore the role of the writer and the form of telling stories in theatre.

If you would like further information about the Attachment Programme or Grass Routes contact the Arts Team Administrator, and if you would like to know more about the Transmissions work contact the Playwriting Officer.

Artistic Director Rachel Kavanaugh
Executive Director Stuart Rogers

Box Office: 0121 236 4455
Administration: 0121 245 2000
www.birmingham-rep.co.uk

Birmingham Repertory Theatre is a registered charity, number 223660

Supported by
ARTS COUNCIL ENGLAND

Birmingham Repertory Theatre Company

Development Officer
Ros Adams

Theatre Manager
Nigel Cairns

Duty Managers
Darren Perry
Nicola Potocka

Sales Manager
Gerard Swift

Sales Team Supervisor
Rebecca Thorndyke

**Sales Development
Supervisor**
Rachel Foster

Sales Team
Anne Bower
Kayleigh Cottam
Sebastian Maynard-Francis
Eileen Minnock
Jonathan Smith

Senior Usher
Brenda Bradley
Thanks to our team of casual
Box Office staff, ushers and
Firemen

Stage Door Reception
Tracey Dolby
Robert Flynn
Neil Hill
Julie Plumb

Building Services Officer
Colin Williamson

Building Services Assistant
John Usowicz

**Cleaning by
We Clean Limited**

Head of Production
Tomas Wright

Production Manager
Milorad Zakula

Production Assistant
Hayley Seddon

Head of Stage
Adrian Bradley

Deputy Head of Stage
Kevin Smith

Stage Technicians
Mario Fortuin
Rosie Williams
Charlie Lee

Head of Lighting
Andrew Fidgeon

Deputy Head of Lighting
Phil Swoffer

Lighting Technicians
Anthony Aston
Simon Bond
Charlie Lee

Head of Sound
Dan Hoole

Deputy Head of Sound
Clive Meldrum

Company Manager
Ruth Morgan

Workshop Supervisor
Margaret Rees

Construction Coordinator
Oliver Shapley

**Deputy Workshop
Supervisor**
Simon Fox

Head Scenic Artist
Christopher Tait

Properties And Armourer
Alan Bennett

Head of Wardrobe
Sue Nightingale

Wardrobe Assistants
Lara Bradbeer
Melanie Francis
Brenda Huxtable
Debbie Williams

Head of Wigs and Make-up
Andrew Whiteoak

**With thanks to the following
volunteers**
Student REPresentatives

REP Archivist
Horace Gillis

FIRST PERSON SHOOTER

Paul Jenkins

Characters

CAPTAIN JONES / NUGGET
ADE
MAGGIE
TOM

Note

*All directions in **bold** are intended to be shown as text onstage. The default suggestion is military/computer game 'videprinter' live text.*

A forward slash (/) in the text indicates the point at which the next speaker interrupts, overlapping.

This text went to press before the end of rehearsals and so may differ slightly from the play as performed.

1.1

SAS Training Camp.
Brecon Beacons, UK.
Day 1.
19:30.

CAPTAIN JONES. Good news first – we got a military coup in
North Korea, pro-democracy rebels have stormed the people's
palace. Happy days – if it weren't for the missing warheads
on the black market. Then there's Mohammed Zarqawi – the
new pin-up beard for Al-Qaeda. Intel reports he's shopping
for a suitcase nuke to go walkabout. Just another day at the
office. Bad news is we got a newbie, fresh out of training…

ADE *hunched in front of a monitor, gamepad in hand.*

How did a n00b like you pass selection? Take one of the rifles
from the table.

Press P to pick up SA80 Assault Rifle.

You know the drill. Go to station 1 and aim down the range.

Press L1 to aim your weapon.

Shoot the target aiming down the sights.

Press R1 to fire your weapon.

Machine-gun fire.

Now, firing from the hip – hit the targets as they pop up, fast
as you can.

Short bursts of machine-gun fire.

Proper good job, mate. Using your knife is faster than
reloading – there's a watermelon on the table, walk over and
knife it.

Press R3 to attack with melee weapon.

Lovely – your fruit-killing skills will come in handy.

Gentlemen, the cargo-ship mission is a go. Intel has located the warhead for the suitcase nuke in the Persian Gulf. It's on a South Korean freighter with security detail on board. Rules of engagement – crew expendable.

Throb of a helicopter engine.

Gazelle special-ops helicopter.
The Persian Gulf.

That's a positive ID on the ship with the nuke. Rappel down to the deck and rush to position 1. Then storm the stairs to position 2. Grab the rope when you're ready.

Press R to rappel down the rope.

Lock and load. Go go go! Hit the targets!

Two bursts of machine-gun fire – screams of dying men.

Bridge secure. Position 2, go.

MAGGIE (*off*). Ade!

CAPTAIN JONES. Guard on the catwalk – sneak up and knife him from behind.

Press R3 to attack with melee weapon.

Slits a throat – choking of a dying man.

MAGGIE (*off*). Adrian – pizza's here!

CAPTAIN JONES. Hostile on the stairs. Stun grenade through the door.

Press L2 to throw stun grenade.

Check those corners. Hit the target.

Burst of machine-gun fire – scream of a dying man.

Sweet dreams – crew quarters clear.

MAGGIE *enters with pizza box.*

Fizz of a Geiger counter.

Getting a strong reading on the Geiger.

MAGGIE. Your favourite – ham and pineapple, extra jalapeños.

CAPTAIN JONES. Take a look at this – lead container covered in Korean.

MAGGIE. Don't tell me – you got a new gun, new level, whatever.

CAPTAIN JONES. Secure the package and get out.

Press S to secure the suitcase nuke.

MAGGIE *wafts the pizza under* ADE*'s nose.*

MAGGIE. Is his nose working or are all his senses absorbed in the virtual battlefield?

CAPTAIN JONES. Two bogeys on the radar – coming in fast.

MAGGIE. Here's the deal – you eat up here, then we play two-player.

CAPTAIN JONES. Enemy aircraft inbound – secure the package.

ADE. Can't play two-player.

MAGGIE. It speaks.

CAPTAIN JONES. We gotta move, soldier!

MAGGIE. Why's he getting ratty with you?

ADE. Jets coming to fry us and you're distracting me.

MAGGIE. You're drooling on the gamepad – eat the pizza and I'll kill some baddies.

ADE. You'll rinse my KDR.

MAGGIE. In human-speak?

CAPTAIN JONES. Enemy aircraft inbound.

ADE. Kill-death ratio, since when you interested?

MAGGIE. Like to know what my boy does all night to inflate the bags under his eyes. Look out – man in a beard with a gun.

Burst of machine-gun fire – scream of a dying man.

Ugh! Bit gruesome. Who are they?

ADE. Commies and insurgents with nukes.

MAGGIE. Fair enough.

5

CAPTAIN JONES. Grab the container – move!

MAGGIE. Come on – paid good money for that pizza.

ADE. You could cook, wouldn't eat take-away all the time.

MAGGIE. Very welcome to make up for any lack you perceive in the kitchen.

CAPTAIN JONES. Get topside – double time.

MAGGIE. Show me how to play and I'll buy the latest Jamie Oliver.

ADE. You're a total n00b.

MAGGIE. I'm a n00b? What's that supposed to mean?

ADE. Want to get in a decent clan, you'll frak my KDR.

MAGGIE. Get the gist of that, not nice, Ade. Talking of not nice, your dad called – he wants you to go visit.

ADE. You talk to him.

Machine-gun fire – scream of a dying man.

MAGGIE. I'll end up doing that to him. Come on – quick game, then I'll go.

ADE. Didn't even knock – I'll put a lock on that door.

She puts down the pizza, leaving…

MAGGIE. Be in front of the plasma, alone, again. Not a guilt-trip – this n00b would just like some QT with her son. Watching a movie, gaming, not fussy…

ADE. Surfing Guardian Soulmates for a new life-partner.

Jets swoop overhead.

A massive explosion.

CAPTAIN JONES. We've been hit – run for the deck, move move move!

MAGGIE. Thanks, Ade – I'll get back to that now.

MAGGIE *closes the door.*

CAPTAIN JONES. You're on your own now, son – multiple KIAs.

6

Buzz of the helicopter blades.

There's the helicopter – jump for it!

Press X to jump for the helicopter.

ADE. Shit.

CAPTAIN JONES. Don't worry, soldier – nobody makes the first jump.

Respawn in 5.
4.
3.
2.
1.
0.

1.2

TOM, *with laptop, wrapping up his presentation.*

Malvern Technology Centre.
Worcestershire, UK.
Day 2.
13:48.

TOM. In conclusion – the network currently handles speeds to 120 mph, but new high-speed links from London to Scotland will mean velocities up to 215 mph. To maintain safety and performance, and assess the extra mechanical stress, a new paradigm in track metrology is required. The Compact hybrid Laser radar and Thermal Imaging System, or 'COLTIS'…

COLTIS – COmpact hybrid Laser radar & Thermal Imaging System.

… offers unparalleled analysis of our rail infrastructure. The thermal imager detects friction hotspots, and 3D laser radar quantifies the nature of any deterioration. The lightweight design of COLTIS facilitates mounting on a commercial UAV…

UAV – Unmanned Air Vehicle.

… far more cost-effective than current equipment, which requires a full-size helicopter. This, ladies and gentlemen, is the technology our new public transport system will be built on, ensuring speed and safety for the future of rail travel. If you have any questions I'll be very happy to try and answer them.

MAGGIE. Tom – do you mind?

TOM. Not at all – Maggie Cole, our new business group manager.

MAGGIE. You say COLTIS will be cheaper – how do in-service costs compare with conventional track analysis?

TOM. There was a slide with the breakdown.

MAGGIE. No – there wasn't.

He struggles with his PowerPoint.

TOM. Here somewhere… about twenty-five per cent cheaper over a five-year period.

MAGGIE. And initial procurement?

TOM. Depends if it's initial prototypes or mass manufacture… it's all on the slide…

MAGGIE. Give us a rough idea.

TOM. Here it is…

The wrong slide pops up.

That's not it.

MAGGIE. Let's mingle in the foyer for the buffet lunch and we can get those details out.

TOM *shuts his laptop.*

TOM. Yes. Thank you.

MAGGIE. Great presentation.

TOM. Sorry, bit jittery, then…

MAGGIE. No puddles on the floor – always a good sign.

TOM. Wrong slide.

MAGGIE. Didn't mean to sabotage you – they only spit the dummy when they see the figures.

TOM. The rest was okay?

MAGGIE. Like the acronym COLTIS – feral, inquisitive, suits the product. I can sell that acronym.

TOM. Bit techie was it?

MAGGIE. All good – bore them rigid with the tech, slap them in the face with the operating advantages.

TOM. Two guys first out for the buffet – Virgin Rail, I should go schmooze.

MAGGIE. No, Tom – you've earned a couple of hours in the pub.

TOM. I don't mind talking to them.

MAGGIE. Leave this to me – not got MBA after my name for nothing.

TOM. Mediocre But Arrogant.

She doesn't get it.

Acronym for MBA.

MAGGIE. Not heard that one.

TOM. Ignore me – mild Tourette's.

MAGGIE. Haven't been through the medical files yet.

TOM. Not really – it was a joke.

MAGGIE. The insulting acronym or the inappropriate quip?

TOM. Both. Sorry, bit wired still.

MAGGIE. Go have that drink – get them to sign, I'll treat us both to a Snickers.

TOM. Motivation skills – that MBA. (*Picks up his bag.*) Slip them a brochure on the way out. See you tomorrow…

MAGGIE. Long as I make sunrise with all four limbs.

TOM. Something up?

MAGGIE. Keep waking in a sweat – checking my legs and vital organs are still there.

TOM. Nightmares?

MAGGIE. Twenty-four-hour counter-insurgency upstairs.

TOM. Noisy neighbours?

MAGGIE. Teenage-son computer-game stuff.

TOM. I'm a son, formerly teenage, still gaming, if you wanted a professional opinion?

MAGGIE. Didn't know you were a gamer?

TOM. Jet Set Willy, Ant Attack, the holidays I lost banging the keyboard to Daley Thompson's Decathlon.

MAGGIE. Not sure he's playing those.

TOM. Old Spectrum games, got an emulator for my PC. Also 360 and PS3. What's he playing?

MAGGIE. He's got lots of different guns, a knife, all kinds of bombs and stuff.

TOM. Narrows it down a bit. Not.

MAGGIE. Thousands of insurgents trying to kill him – so he has to kill them.

TOM. Absolutely no evidence linking computer games and violent behaviour. If there was, I'd be a homicidal maniac – and I'm not.

MAGGIE. Glad to hear it, Tom.

TOM. Except the one taxi driver I dragged out of his cab at knifepoint. Grand Theft Auto, it's a game.

MAGGIE. He called me a n00b.

TOM. Slang for somebody doesn't know how to play.

MAGGIE. Said something about a kill-death ratio, so he could join a gang?

TOM. Clan – team of players, online.

MAGGIE. Really do know your onions?

TOM. Twenty-five years' active service. Have you played?

MAGGIE. Bites my head off every time I suggest a two-player.

TOM. Can't say I used to game with my mum, God knows what she'd think now.

MAGGIE. Bit squeamish is she?

TOM. Ran a veggie-burger stand on Greenham Common.

MAGGIE. Must have made a fortune.

TOM. She didn't charge for them – volunteer for CND. So war games, first person shooters…

MAGGIE. Bit of a no-no.

TOM. If you're worried, we could have a game online, multiplayer.

MAGGIE. That's very kind, Tom.

TOM (*looks over*). Virgin boys have filled their boots – slip them my contact details.

MAGGIE. Why don't you pop round for dinner some time?

TOM. Come round to your house?

MAGGIE. You could meet Adrian, set it up face to face. If it doesn't sound too weird.

TOM. No, no – nothing weird about that. Last manager very hands-off, everything by e-mail. She dated a guy in IT – they never actually met.

MAGGIE. Well, I'm hands-on.

TOM. Long as I'm not intruding, stepping on Ade's dad's toes?

MAGGIE. We're separated.

TOM. Didn't realise, sorry.

MAGGIE. I'm not, why should you be? When's good?

TOM. Any evening, except Tuesdays – badminton club.

MAGGIE. Ade'll be really chuffed to meet a fellow gamer.

She takes a small scrap of paper, a pen.

I'll write down the address.

TOM. You could mail me.

MAGGIE. Only take a second.

TOM. No – you can't, I mean I can't, small pieces of paper.

MAGGIE. Small pieces of paper?

TOM. Have this thing with small pieces of paper.

MAGGIE. What thing?

TOM. Panic attacks – papyrophobia, fear of little pieces of paper.

MAGGIE. You're joking, right?

TOM. Brainstorming session in avionics last week, everyone had to write twenty ideas on different coloured Post-its. I blacked out, came round in sickbay.

MAGGIE. That's rather charming, Tom.

> MAGGIE *writes on* TOM*'s hand.*

TOM. Brilliant. (*Leaving.*) They've gone.

MAGGIE. Not to worry, I'll arrange a conference call first thing.

TOM. Let me know how it goes – want a Snickers on my desk by the end of the week.

1.3

USAF base.
Nevada, USA.
Day 6.
20:37.

CAPTAIN JONES. Gentlemen – intel reports Zarqawi has salvaged the warhead from the wreck. We've tracked him to a suspect bomb factory in the Yemen. This is a joint operation with our friends and allies, the US Air Force.

Low drone of an aeroplane engine.

Reaper UAV.
Southern Yemen.

You are to provide UAV remote air support for SAS ground troops. Do not fire on units marked with a strobe – they're friendlies, all other targets can be assumed hostile.

8 x Hellfire missiles.
GBU 500lb smart bomb.
Press C to cycle through weapons.

ADE *sits at a dining table with handheld game console.*

An open laptop, bottle of wine, glasses, cutlery.

Confirm you see the mosque in the town. You are not authorised to level sites of worship – beefs up the locals. Repeat – do not fire directly on the mosque. Hostiles are in the compound next door.

Hellfire missile selected.

Clear to engage enemy personnel.

Press R1 to fire.

A missile launch.

Direct hit. They're making a run for it.

A missile launch.

You got 'em. Taking cover by the trees.

The doorbell rings.

MAGGIE (*off*). Can you get that?

A missile launch.

CAPTAIN JONES. Light 'em up. Target reset.

MAGGIE *enters.*

MAGGIE. Asked you to lay the table, Ade.

Doorbell rings.

CAPTAIN JONES. One of the vehicles is moving.

Smart bomb selected.

A distant explosion.

MAGGIE *answers the door to* TOM, *carrying a box in a plastic bag.*

MAGGIE. Did you find it alright?

TOM. My favourite part of town. Near the hills, nice and leafy, next to the college. Is that where Ade...?

MAGGIE. No, didn't want to move him – final year, exams. He's applying to do Classics at uni.

TOM. Wow – Classics. Is that literature or something?

MAGGIE. Penguin Classics – that's what I thought. Tell him, Ade.

A distant explosion.

CAPTAIN JONES. Firing too close to those friendlies – watch for the strobes.

MAGGIE. Roman and Greek – art, philosophy. Got this fab Ancient Greek teacher, so we wanted him to stay.

TOM. Where's that then?

MAGGIE. Oxford.

TOM. Bit of a school run.

MAGGIE. Ade boards. Suspended for a week – caught him with a bifta.

CAPTAIN JONES. We got a runner here.

Hellfire missile selected.

TOM. A what?

MAGGIE. Spliff, joint. Personally I think you need a bit of skunk to fully appreciate the Classics.

A missile launch.

CAPTAIN JONES. You got him.

MAGGIE. Can I take your coat?

TOM. Thanks. Any news from Virgin?

MAGGIE. Only one rule in this house – work stays on the doorstep. No schoolwork, no work work, no nothing.

TOM. No housework – just like my place.

MAGGIE. Is it that obvious?

TOM. No – I was…

MAGGIE. That sense of humour will get you into trouble.

TOM. Been tinkering with the optical amplifier in the lab, thirty per cent bump in range, thought Virgin should…

MAGGIE. Breaking the rule, Tom.

CAPTAIN JONES. Hostiles in cover by the trees.

TOM. Was going to bring a bottle of wine or something.

Presents his plastic bag.

MAGGIE. Enough wine here to float the Pope.

She takes the box out of the bag.

A missile launch.

CAPTAIN JONES. You nailed 'em.

TOM (*re: the box*). Same as Ade's, games console, so we can all play online.

MAGGIE. I couldn't possibly – they're hundreds of pounds.

TOM. It's a spare, came free with my broadband.

MAGGIE. Thank you so much. Adrian, look what Tom brought us.

CAPTAIN JONES. SAS units have cleared the compound, no sign of the suitcase nuke.

MAGGIE. Excuse my mute son – fill him with cheap plonk and you can't shut him up. Not vegetarian or anything?

TOM. No – long as it's cooked properly.

CAPTAIN JONES. Enemy personnel on the road.

MAGGIE. Turn that off now, Ade.

A missile launch.

TOM. Had a dose of gastroenteritis, dodgy chicken from a rotisserie. Thought I was going to die – projectile liquids, both ends, blood in my stools for a month.

MAGGIE. Don't spare us the gory details.

TOM. Seven million bacteria in an undercooked chicken – what are we having?

MAGGIE. A roast… chicken.

A missile launch.

CAPTAIN JONES. You got him, missile hit two feet in front of him.

MAGGIE. If you'd rather something else?

TOM. Overuse of antibiotics has led to a huge increase in bacterial infections – but as long as it's cooked properly.

MAGGIE. This is free-range, organic.

TOM. They don't use *any* antibiotics – can be even worse.

CAPTAIN JONES. Armoured vehicle leaving the mosque. The bomb factory must've been there.

Smart bomb selected.

MAGGIE. Turn that off now, Ade – we can play after dinner.

TOM. How much does it weigh?

CAPTAIN JONES. Zarqawi is escaping with the nuke!

A distant explosion.

MAGGIE. Four, four-and-a-half pounder?

TOM. Twenty minutes per pound plus one – that's an hour and forty. What temperature is the oven?

MAGGIE. It's a recipe on the net… (*Checks laptop.*) One ninety.

TOM. Fahrenheit or centigrade? And the preheat?

MAGGIE. Before you put it in the oven?

TOM. You did preheat?

MAGGIE. There's a little C next to it. What time did we put it in, Ade?

CAPTAIN JONES. Zarqawi is escaping with the nuke!

A distant explosion.

TOM. Think I have the solution.

TOM *takes a digital gizmo from his pocket.*

CAPTAIN JONES. Have to do better than that, soldier.

MAGGIE. What is it?

TOM. Digital meat thermometer.

MAGGIE. Right.

TOM. Stick the probe in the inner thigh, but *not* touching the bone, must be over eighty-two, centigrade.

MAGGIE. I just stick it in?

TOM. Middle of the meat – *not* touching the bone, very important.

MAGGIE *goes to the kitchen with meat thermometer.*

TOM *and* ADE *transfixed by the game.*

CAPTAIN JONES. Zarqawi is escaping with the nuke!

A distant explosion.

Have to do better than that, soldier.

MAGGIE (*off*). Pour some wine if you like.

TOM *and* ADE *transfixed by the game.*

CAPTAIN JONES. Zarqawi is escaping with the nuke!

MAGGIE (*off*). I won't ask you again, Ade – turn that off!

ADE *turns off his handheld,* CAPTAIN JONES *disappears.*

An awkward silence.

Now behave like a normal human being and make small talk with Tom.

ADE. Always carry a digital meat thermometer round with you?

TOM. If I'm eating out… yes.

MAGGIE (*off*). Tell him about the little pieces of paper.

TOM. I have an interesting condition – it's called papyrophobia.

ADE. What's that – fear of dads?

TOM. Phobia of small pieces of paper.

ADE. Cool.

MAGGIE (*off*). Tell us about your hippy mum, she sounds like fun.

TOM. Bit of a mystery, my mother – reads the *Daily Mail* and the *Morning Star* alternate days. She's the only pro-life CND member I know – makes sense if you think about it.

MAGGIE (*off*). It says ninety-three point five.

TOM. Centigrade?

MAGGIE. There's a little C next to it.

TOM. Heard about the new one from Intelligent Arts? Modern War: Future Warrior – the most authentic warfare experience ever. Preordered a copy, booked a week's holiday, don't tell your mum.

ADE (*shouts*). Mum – Tom says he's taking a week off to play a computer game.

MAGGIE (*off*). I'm dishing – there in a mo.

TOM. Same programmers that design the simulators, for the Army.

ADE. What simulators?

TOM. Virtual infantry trainers – they're using a beta version of Future Warrior. VR units, the works.

ADE. How do you know?

TOM. Old mate from college does the graphics. Programmed all the deaths – two hunded and seventy-six ways of dying.

TOM *dies stupidly,* ADE *ignores him.*

MAGGIE *brings through the chicken, burnt to a cinder.*

MAGGIE. Those are roast potatoes and that's… parsnips, they're a different shape.

ADE. Totally nuked.

MAGGIE. The oven was on two seventy. Centigrade.

ADE. This romantic dinner is KIA.

MAGGIE. What's that supposed to mean?

TOM. Killed in action. Dead.

MAGGIE. Did you turn up the oven, Ade?

ADE. Don't blame me you can't roast a chicken.

MAGGIE. Ade thinks every man I see outside work is a date.

ADE. Any autistic dude carries a meat thermometer is down with me.

MAGGIE. Adrian!

ADE. Won't have to worry with your cooking.

TOM. Nothing fishy going on – I'm just relieved your mum isn't half the bitch our last manager was.

MAGGIE. Thanks, Tom.

TOM. I mean – we're work colleagues, friends, that's all.

ADE. Going to order an Indian.

MAGGIE. Bring through the menu. You can set up the console on the plasma while we're waiting.

ADE *goes into the lounge.*

The little shit. Should've guessed he'd try something, been teasing me about internet dating.

TOM. Well, it is a teaseable offence, I keep sensitive information like that under wraps.

MAGGIE. You do internet dating?

TOM. Me? No.

MAGGIE. You know your eyes go up and left when you lie?

TOM. Teach that on the MBA, do they?

MAGGIE. Day one. What was the last date you went on?

TOM. Don't actually go on dates. Good, though – pick your favourites, feels like your own private harem.

MAGGIE. Show me.

TOM. What?

MAGGIE. The website, your profile – show me your harem!

TOM. I don't think so.

MAGGIE. Come on – you show me yours, I'll show you mine.

TOM finds the website, hesitates.

TOM. Forgotten my password.

MAGGIE. Eyes.

He types it in.

TOM. So – these are my favourites.

MAGGIE. Wow – they're beautiful, Tom.

TOM. Problem being, there's another page, the ones that have chosen me as *their* favourite.

MAGGIE. Oh God. I see. Guys as well?

TOM. No, those are girls.

MAGGIE. What if you send the more female-looking ones messages?

TOM. I don't.

MAGGIE. Why not?

TOM. Look at them – the ones I like will laugh in my face.

MAGGIE. Nobody's going to laugh in your face – that's the point.

TOM. Let's see yours then.

MAGGIE. I'm not that desperate – not yet.

TOM. You said you did.

MAGGIE. I go sit in a bar on my own and neck sambucas forlornly.

ADE (*enters with remote*). Plasma's not picking up the AV.

MAGGIE. I don't know – ask Tom.

TOM. Can have a look if you like?

ADE *holds out the remote,* TOM *takes it through.*

MAGGIE. Go on – he won't bite.

ADE *goes through,* MAGGIE *clicks the mouse, writes a message.*

TOM *and* ADE *come back.*

TOM. Plugged the console into the ethernet down here, better bandwidth, less lag.

MAGGIE *looks blank.*

Faster connection – better kill-death ratio for Ade.

MAGGIE. That's what we want.

TOM. Why don't I dash home – can have a multiplayer online?

MAGGIE. What about dinner?

TOM. I'll pick up something on the way back, we can eat and play, chat on the headsets.

MAGGIE. If you don't mind. What do you say, Ade?

ADE: Sure – let's pwn some n00bs.

ADE. Sure – let's pwn some n00bs.

1.4

First Person Shooter – a beginner's guide.

CAPTAIN JONES. Let's pwn some n00bs.

Pwn.

To own – verb, spelt P, W, N… To kill, to annihilate, to totally dominate your opponent. Pronounced as O but spelt with P, what originated as a typo by chronic gamers, is now legendary in the gaming lexicon. If you have *pwned* another player – the *pwnage* unleashed upon them may be due to the fact they are a *n00b.*

n00b.

Noun, spelt N, zero, zero, B – *n00b*. Got to admit there's a
ring to it. Often mistook as an abbreviation of 'newbie' – a
novice, new to the game – the real meaning of *n00b* goes far
deeper than this. The true *n00b* is not only ignorant, but
unwilling or incapable of learning. Hence the justification of
total or *uber-pwnage*...

Uber-pwnage.

... of this gaming underclass. For example: 'I totally *pwned*
those *n00bs*' would roughly translate as: 'I completely
annihilated those morons'. The *n00b*, in response to this
onslaught, may resort to defensive tactics, or *camping*:

Camping.

Hiding in a particular spot, sniping at random players from a
safe distance. *Campers* are the scum of first person shooters,
parasites of the virtual battlefield, *uber-n00bs* in contravention
of the warrior ethic of serious gamers. After *pwning n00bs*,
camping or otherwise, it is customary to celebrate by *tea-
bagging*.

Tea-bagging.

Some of you may be familiar with this already. Suckling of
the genitalia, namely the balls, or while gaming – dunking
them into the face of the recently deceased, as one might a
Tetley or PG tips tea bag into a mug. This ritual evolved with
the ability to crouch, allowing your avatar to squat down and
tea-bag the enemy corpse. But you're not the only one trying
to *pwn* all the *n00bs* and *tea-bag* them. Your turn will come to
be *pwned* like a total *n00b* and be humiliated by *tea-bagging*.
But don't despair, it's not the end – within seconds you will
respawn.

Respawn.

A freshly cloned cyber-warrior, with laser-sighted AK-47 and
frag grenades, will materialise at a portal nearby. In short – find
the *n00bs*, *pwn* the *n00bs*, *tea-bag* them, get *pwned*, get *tea-
bagged*, *respawn*. In no event resort to *camping* – I repeat,
under no circumstances go *camping*. Now you're ready to play.

Team Deathmatch beginning in 5.

4.

3.

2.

1.

0.

> ADE, TOM *and* MAGGIE *– hunched over gamepads.*

> *They speak over the din of battle via headsets.*

TOM. See the mosque with the smoke coming out of it?

ADE. Roger that – light machine guns and mortars.

TOM. What launchers we got?

ADE. Stinger missile and the UAV.

MAGGIE. What's a UAV again?

TOM. Unmanned air vehicle. Recon – so we can see them on the map.

ADE. See them from the tracer fire.

TOM. Ade – take a snipe from the roof – two more kills and we get an air strike.

ADE. Not sniping anyone.

MAGGIE. Listen. I've got a plan. Why don't we run out, and start shooting?

TOM. Don't be a n00b, Maggie.

MAGGIE. Been playing for five hours – hardly call me a n00b.

TOM. I'll lay down suppressing fire. You two sneak round and take their flanks.

ADE. That's camping talk.

TOM. What about the UAV then? Not going anywhere without recon.

ADE. Okay – Tom – take the UAV up the roof. Mum, when they see the launch they'll take a pop – you see anything…

MAGGIE. Boom. Head shot.

ADE. When they appear on the map – we attack.

Enemy UAV online.

TOM. They beat us to it!

ADE. Now they can see us.

MAGGIE. LEEROY JENKINS!

    Machine-gun fire as MAGGIE *runs out into the fray.*

TOM. Maggie – what you doing?

MAGGIE. Saw it on YouTube.

TOM. Uber-n00b behaviour, Maggie.

    Shouting in Arabic from the distance, return fire.

ADE. Forget the UAV – let's move.

MAGGIE. Taking heavy fire – where are you guys?

Enemy Apache inbound.

TOM. They're on a killstreak! Find some cover.

    The helicopter swoops low, spitting bullets.

ADE. Tom – take it out with the Stinger.

TOM. Jeez, that was close…

MAGGIE. It's over here, Tom, right above me.

TOM. Good shooting spot in this bunker.

MAGGIE. You're going the wrong way.

ADE. Take it out, Tom.

TOM. I'm there. Locking on.

    Fires a rocket.

ADE. How did you miss that?

TOM. Sorry, guys.

    The tinkle of metal on concrete.

ADE. Mum, grenade.

MAGGIE. What do I do?

TOM. Press R2 to throw it back.

An explosion.

BadMuvva68 KIA.

ADE. Pwned.

TOM. They're making a run for you – must be low on ammo.

ADE. Either that or…

MAGGIE. I respawned, where am I?

TOM. Right here – getting a good tea-bagging.

MAGGIE. That's disgusting – Adrian, don't look.

ADE. Picked up another Stinger. Locking on.

Whoosh of a rocket, an almighty explosion.

The helicopter whines, crashes.

You killed RazorPig.

TOM. Black Hawk down!

MAGGIE. Must have spawned on a new map. There's nothing on my radar.

TOM. You're in n00b heaven.

The rumble of an aircraft.

ADE. What's that? Tom, you call an air strike?

TOM. No. Sounds like a…

Enemy AC-130 gunship inbound.

The plane swoops low over the battlefield.

ADE. They're on another killstreak!

A deafening roar, a blanket of bombs.

TOM. Get to the bunker – quick.

MAGGIE. I'm on the roof. I can see you guys.

ADE. I'm taking hits. Do or die.

ADE *charges heroically at the enemy.*

You killed Tit0n87.
You killed Zombie Nosh.
You killed madSkillZ.

Where are you, Tom?

TOM. Just stocking up on ammo.

n00bassassin93 KIA.

MAGGIE. Messy – blew your legs clean off.

TOM. Wait till that gunship's gone and then – uber-pwnage.

Deathmatch score limit reached – you were defeated!

Definitely next game.

ADE. My KDR can't take any more of this.

MAGGIE. Come on, Ade, don't be a killjoy.

ADE. You n00bs crack on.

MAGGIE. One more Team Deathmatch.

ADE. Got some dude called Plato to read.

ADE *disappears offline.*

MAGGIE. Would've been alright if we got our UAV up.

TOM. Or you hadn't gone Rambo on us.

MAGGIE. Five hours of my life well spent.

TOM. You can spend days, not eating, not sleeping, hanging on for the toilet till you unlock the next weapon.

MAGGIE. Think he likes you.

TOM. Not sure about that.

MAGGIE. Nice for him to have a gaming buddy.

TOM. Sure he's got plenty online.

MAGGIE. I mean a real one.

TOM. Maggie?

MAGGIE. Yes, Tom?

TOM. Did you send a message from me, on that website?

MAGGIE. Just a little one. Was that very naughty?

TOM. They wrote back, I've got a date.

1.5

Army Careers.
Worcester, UK.
Day 9.
16:22.

A desktop computer.

NUGGET. Application process takes about three months to complete. We'll watch some DVDs today – like what you see, we'll book a full entrance test. Says here you want to apply for infantry soldier.

ADE. Roger that.

NUGGET. Talked to Sergeant Hammond online?

ADE. Affirmative.

NUGGET. He explained what an infantry soldier does?

ADE. I got all the intel.

NUGGET. The intel?

ADE. Operate worldwide in a professional combat unit, sir. From peacekeeping and disaster relief, to full-scale war, sir.

NUGGET. You taking the piss?

ADE. No.

NUGGET. Coz recruits don't talk like that. Not till you're enlisted and we tell you to talk like that. How old are you?

ADE. Seventeen.

NUGGET. GCSEs?

ADE. English, English Lit, Biology, Chemistry, Physics, Economics, Computer Science and Ancient Greek.

NUGGET. That'll come in handy. You seen the movie *300*?

ADE. No.

NUGGET. Three hundred Greeks – against the entire Persian army.

ADE. Spartans.

NUGGET. Same difference, three hundred Spartans against the entire Persian army – what do you think happened?

ADE. Spartans beat the Persians.

NUGGET. No, come on, millions of Persians, against three hundred.

ADE. Spartans win.

NUGGET. I'll give you one more guess.

ADE. Persians lose.

NUGGET. Yes, no, Spartans *nearly* beat the Persians. Outnumbered hundreds of thousands.

ADE. You said millions.

NUGGET. Historical records vary – fuck of a lot of Persians and not many Spartans. But then your Spartans had the phalanx.

ADE. I know.

NUGGET. The original combat unit, every soldier protects his fellow with his own shield – what being infantryman's all about. What do you mean you know?

ADE. Did it in Ancient Greek.

NUGGET. Play any sport?

ADE. Used to run – cross-country.

NUGGET. You'll need to pass a fitness test, so you better start running across the country again.

ADE. Has anyone ever told you…

NUGGET. Yes.

ADE. It's uncanny.

NUGGET. Truth is, I play the game a lot, weeks at a time, like you kids do, love it so much, that character in particular, I modelled myself on him.

ADE. Did you?

NUGGET. Affirmative.

ADE. You modelled yourself on a character out of a computer game?

NUGGET. What do you think?

ADE. No – you probably didn't.

NUGGET. No – I probably didn't, maybe they modelled him on me.

ADE. Thought you might be a consultant. They do that – hire real soldiers to help design it, put their avatar in the game.

NUGGET. Play a lot of computer games?

ADE. I pwn them.

NUGGET. You collect them?

ADE. Kill them, dominate them, the n00bs.

NUGGET. n00bs? Newbies?

ADE. No.

NUGGET. What then?

ADE. n00bs – total ignorants.

NUGGET. You kill, you dominate – the total ignorants?

ADE. That's what we say.

NUGGET. Well, we don't, that is most definitely not what we say, not in public. Why do you want to join the Army?

ADE. Stop the terrorists – making suitcase nukes.

NUGGET. You got all the intel.

ADE. Hate them – camping n00bs. Civilian targets – uber-campers.

NUGGET. Not talking tents and Boy Scouts are you?

ADE. Like some douche on a twenty-five killstreak, camping the respawn portal, drops the nuke, game over, uber-n00b, terrorists the same.

NUGGET. Haven't the foggiest what you're banging on about. Take that, see you when you land back on planet Earth.

ADE. What is it?

NUGGET. A brochure – read the words, turn the page – there's more words.

ADE. Have online – I'm ready to join.

NUGGET. Ready to join a team like no other? To live and work in a hostile environment and defeat a heavily armed enemy? Ready to be stretched further than you thought possible? Pushed to the limit, physically and mentally? Ready to be shouted at and shot at? Witness scenes of injury, death and devastation?

ADE. What I've always dreamed of.

NUGGET. Make friends for life – closer than any brother.

ADE. Whatever.

NUGGET. Book you in for an entrance test then. Next Tuesday?

ADE. As part of the test – do I have to go on the simulators?

NUGGET. Simulators?

ADE. Combat simulators.

NUGGET. Don't know anything about that.

ADE. Virtual infantry trainers – I know you got them.

NUGGET. You want to go on the simulators?

ADE. Only if I have to – as part of the test.

NUGGET. Tell you what – why don't we do it now.

ADE. Here?

NUGGET. Why not?

ADE. You got it on your computer?

NUGGET. On the desktop.

ADE. I'm ready. Let's do it.

> NUGGET *rolls up his sleeve, puts his elbow on the desk.*

What's that?

NUGGET. That's the test.

ADE. What about the simulator?

NUGGET. Forget the simulator – this is the real thing.

ADE. Said you had it on your desktop.

NUGGET. It is on my desk top. Pass the test – you can go on the simulators.

ADE. That's not fair.

NUGGET. Need recruits ready for the physical challenge – prepared to have a go.

ADE. I'll never beat you.

NUGGET. Physical test isn't as vital as the mental test – you just failed.

ADE. Get me on the simulators – I'll show you what I can do.

NUGGET. I finished basic in '82, straight off to the Falklands. South America – rum, samba, chicas, happy days, I thought. Frozen turd of an island. Nothing there but sheep and Argie conscripts. Dug in a big bastard hill, trenches, miles of them. Dream about that hill every night. Do you know what's at the top of it?

ADE. A firefight.

NUGGET. Teenagers' brains steaming in their helmets. Have to sleep with that every night.

ADE. Sounds mental.

NUGGET. We lost two hundred and fifty-two on that useless rock – 'bout the same as topped themselves after coming home.

ADE. I still want to sign.

NUGGET. We can teach you how to kill, son, can't teach you how to deal with the consequences. For that – we need recruits who show signs of maturity. You haven't shown that today, Adrian.

ADE. Give me a chance.

NUGGET. Sorry, son – you don't have the necessary to become a soldier.

ADE. I'm ready to sign up.

NUGGET. I'm ready for lunch.

1.6

Malvern Technology Centre.
Day 10.
14:32.

MAGGIE. So – good news or the bad news?

TOM. How about just the good news?

MAGGIE. We've been offered a contract for COLTIS.

TOM. That's brilliant! Where's my Snickers?

MAGGIE *opens a drawer – tosses him a Snickers bar.*

MAGGIE. You thought I'd forgotten.

TOM. Had a feeling you'd close those liggers from Virgin. (*Bites victoriously into the bar.*) The sickly salty taste of success!

MAGGIE. Why you think I've got a drawer-full?

TOM. Guessing the bad news is eighty-seven pages of design amendments.

MAGGIE. Afraid you'll have to cancel your camping holiday.

TOM. What camping holiday?

MAGGIE. Holiday you booked – Ade said you were going camping.

TOM. Camping? Did he?

MAGGIE. Need you here for the trial with the MoD next week.

TOM. MoD?

MAGGIE. Virgin didn't go for it.

TOM. Why's the Ministry of Defence interested in upgrading the rail network?

MAGGIE. Very exciting, Tom. They think COLTIS can be adapted for urban radar – to patrol trouble spots remotely.

TOM. Been through all this with the last manager…

MAGGIE. It's light, it's powerful, it's perfect…

TOM. When we were privatised, we had a choice…

MAGGIE. Send a low-flying UAV with COLTIS into a village instead of a soldier…

TOM. Work for military research or this, the commercial wing.

MAGGIE. Save hundreds of lives, Tom.

TOM. I don't want my skills used to develop weapons.

MAGGIE. It's not weapons, Tom, it's imaging, surveillance…

TOM. And targeting.

MAGGIE. We don't know that yet.

TOM. What about Virgin? Why can't we stick to the original plan?

MAGGIE. Not viable – they'd buy a couple of units and we'd be tied up with tech support for peanuts.

TOM. It's specifically designed for civil applications.

MAGGIE. You know how things are – this is the only way I can see COLTIS moving forward.

TOM. My granddad worked on the railways, he was a conscientious objector, went to prison for it. My mum…

MAGGIE. Sold burgers on Greenham Common.

TOM. Gave them away, veggie burgers. If two generations of my family can make that sacrifice…

MAGGIE. Wouldn't say running a veggie-burger stall was much of a sacrifice.

TOM. She's not vegetarian. Sorry, Maggie, it's a definite no on this one.

MAGGIE. I understand, I'd ask Rob and Graham but...

TOM. What would you ask them?

MAGGIE. To prepare COLTIS for the trial.

TOM. They'd refuse, they're my team.

MAGGIE. Exactly, this is your baby. Not just the product, the research and papers you delivered are in a class of their own. Really, Tom – I've been blown away by your work.

TOM. Thank you, but the 'gentleman's not for turning'.

MAGGIE. We're not the only ones developing the technology – this way we get to control what they do with it.

TOM. I don't buy that, someone has to take responsibility for how this is used.

MAGGIE. Couldn't agree more, problem being, if it's not us then who will it be?

TOM. Somebody with less scruples.

MAGGIE. And you're happy to let that happen?

TOM. I'm certainly *not* happy to be the one that puts it out there.

Beat.

MAGGIE. How was the date?

TOM. What date?

MAGGIE. Girl I mailed on the website, thought you were all set up?

TOM. Went over her profile again – decided we weren't compatible.

MAGGIE. She was beautiful.

TOM. She was Australian.

MAGGIE. What's wrong with that?

TOM. Had an Australian girlfriend at college. Started to pick up the accent – I didn't mind but all my mates took the piss.

MAGGIE. Can be irritating.

TOM. Sorry, Maggie, it's a no, simple as that.

MAGGIE. There are lads the same age as Adrian, at war without the right equipment, blown to pieces by IEDs.

TOM. Have you seen *their* equipment? They're lucky if they've got a rifle tied to a moped. As for IEDs, the clue is in the I – *improvised* explosive device. Against Apache helicopters, smart bombs – the most advanced military technology in the world.

MAGGIE. Next time a coffin comes out of a transport plane, I don't want to think – I could've done something about that.

TOM. For every one of our soldiers, they lose dozens, hundreds. What kind of advantage are we looking for here?

MAGGIE *proffers her iPad.*

MAGGIE. Have a look at that.

TOM. I know, they're nice, I'm going to get one.

MAGGIE. The article.

TOM. Don't want to read some teenager's obituary.

MAGGIE. Young para saw his best friend die, head ripped off by a roadside bomb. Went on a rampage through a village…

TOM (*reading*). That's…

MAGGIE. Seventeen civilians, women, children… It's the cycle of violence, Tom. By engaging the enemy remotely we can stop this. Take revenge out of the equation.

TOM. Bloody hell.

MAGGIE. If we can reduce casualties on both sides, don't we have a responsibility to do that? How about I offer you another Snickers on this one?

TOM. Not funny, Maggie – I'm serious about this.

MAGGIE. So am I – this could revolutionise our armed forces. Who says war has to be barbaric?

TOM. I imagine it'll still be pretty uncivilised for them.

MAGGIE. If we're going to get philosophical – we may as well do it properly.

MAGGIE *takes a spliff from her drawer.*

TOM. What's that?

MAGGIE. Confiscated some of Ade's stash.

TOM. You can't smoke that in here.

MAGGIE. Thought we'd go in the car park.

TOM. What about security?

MAGGIE. They might join us for a quick toke.

TOM. Getting me high on drugs won't make me change my mind.

MAGGIE. We'll go back to Virgin. They'll close the department in six months but we'll sleep at night.

TOM. What about Europe? The Germans, spend billions on their railways – it's ready to go.

MAGGIE. Fuck it. Let's go down the pub. Save this for later.

1.7

Breaking news…
UK increases terror threat to 'Critical'.
Breaking news…
UK increases terror threat to 'Critical'.

CAPTAIN JONES. This is not an exercise – repeat, this is not an exercise. Our nemesis has landed, Mohammed Zarqawi has breached UK borders with the suitcase nuke. NCB emergency and decontamination units being mobilised. Zephyr UAV is tracking a rogue radiation source towards central London.

The capital's high street – buses, taxis, horns, cyclists, shoppers…

Thousands of shoppers.

Oxford Street.
London, UK.
Day 11.
19:33.

Our last hope – intel has located an off-duty SAS operative, Christmas shopping.

ADE *hunched over a gamepad.*

Satellite linking to his iPhone.

The phone rings.

ADE. Duty calls. What's up, Jonesy?

CAPTAIN JONES. Sorry to interrupt your Crimbo shop, soldier, if you're stuck for ideas – / talcum powder…

ADE. Talcum powder!

CAPTAIN JONES. What we'll all be this goes belly up. We're just praying you packed a shooter to deal with the crowds.

ADE. Never leave home without it.

Press P to pick up Mini UZI.

CAPTAIN JONES. Intel's got an ID on Zarqawi – he's shaved off his beard, tidying up for his seventy-two virgins. Patching through now.

Ping of a text message.

ADE. I got him.

CAPTAIN JONES. No second chances, soldier – your orders are: / shoot to kill.

ADE. Shoot to kill.

CAPTAIN JONES. Our country is in your hands. Rules of engagement – civilian casualties acceptable.

ADE. Yes, sir!

Press R1 to fire your weapon.

He opens fire.

Screams of shoppers.

Bullets and hysteria increase.

1.8

An ashtray with the butt of a joint.

TOM, *eyes closed.*

MAGGIE *placing the final couple of Rizlas on the floor.*

TOM. Not sure this is a good idea.

MAGGIE. Think of it as immunisation, like a jab.

TOM. That's not helping.

MAGGIE. Tiny dose of the disease to make you resistant.

TOM. Before you've had it – not when you've got it.

MAGGIE. Homeopathy then – same theory.

TOM. Just totally ineffective.

MAGGIE. Okay – open.

TOM. One, two, three, four, five – couple of metres away. Yeah, I can deal with that.

MAGGIE. Is it because they're Rizlas not Post-its?

TOM. Worse if something's written on them or they're scrunched up.

MAGGIE. I reckon you made it up to appear more geeky.

TOM. Why would I do that?

MAGGIE. Geeks are the new conquistadors, Bill Gates, Steve Jobs...

TOM. Suppose – boldly going where no man's gone before.

MAGGIE. So now we up the dosage.

TOM. Definitely not, no.

MAGGIE. Just a wee bit – trust me.

TOM *closes his eyes.*

MAGGIE *takes a pen, scribbles on each Rizla before scrunching them up.*

TOM. What are you doing, Maggie?

MAGGIE. Nearly ready.

TOM. Not scrunching them up are you?

MAGGIE. And – open.

TOM *surveys the Rizlas around his feet, swallows.*

How's that?

TOM *shakes his head.*

You're pretending.

TOM. I can't breathe.

MAGGIE. You're joking.

TOM. Serious, I'm hyperventilating.

MAGGIE. Said you couldn't breathe.

TOM. Quick, Maggie – going to faint.

MAGGIE. What's it worth?

TOM. Anything. Please. I'll do anything.

MAGGIE *takes a deep breath, blows them all away.*

MAGGIE. Owe me two Snickers – need to keep my supplies topped up.

TOM. That was horrible, why did you do that?

MAGGIE. Immersion therapy, totally different approach.

TOM. Got a real wicked streak you have.

MAGGIE. So what was it? What happened?

TOM. Nobody knows. Dad was an electrician, invoice pads everywhere. Bit of a mad genius on the side, plans for crazy inventions scribbled all over the place.

MAGGIE. That's where you get it from.

TOM. Had plans for an engine that ran on sea water.

MAGGIE. Amazing – did he get a patent?

TOM. Also claimed he invented the Apple logo. On holiday in Disneyland – bit into a Golden Delicious and bingo.

MAGGIE. Mickey Mouse?

TOM. Says he kept it in a cool box, got stolen in California.

MAGGIE. Any of his ideas ever get made?

TOM. No.

MAGGIE. Nothing more frustrating than a man doesn't deliver his potential. Tell me about the Aussie.

TOM. Mailed her I got a job on the Hadron Collider.

MAGGIE. Not that one, your girlfriend at college.

TOM. Charlene?

MAGGIE. Come on – what was her real name?

TOM. Part of the reason she emigrated.

MAGGIE. You had an Australian girlfriend called Charlene? Didn't have a Labrador called Bouncer by any chance?

TOM. She was gutted – didn't know it was even bigger over here.

MAGGIE. So what happened?

TOM. That's a curly one.

MAGGIE. Sit back and uncurl my friend.

TOM. It was good, then it was really good, then it got worse, then we never spoke to each other again.

MAGGIE. Funny – that happened to me once.

TOM. Very much in love, end of my PhD, we, she got pregnant. Rather baffled by this – about to leap from academia into the real world. I said something like – your call, whatever you want, I'm one hundred per cent behind you, coward that I am. Went to the clinic, took my handheld, played some Pacman, came home. Things were never the same again.

MAGGIE. That's a bit sad. Ever wish you hadn't?

TOM. No. My accent was getting really bad, sounded like I was always asking a question. How about you?

MAGGIE. Had all mine – and one's enough, believe me.

TOM. Ever wish you hadn't?

MAGGIE. I can't imagine life without Ade.

TOM. He's a good kid.

MAGGIE. Do worry sometimes… maybe I've been selfish.

TOM. In what way?

MAGGIE. If he misses having a man around. Computer games, snooker, paintballing – I don't have the genes for it.

TOM. I'd say you do a damn fine job.

MAGGIE. Perhaps that's just me projecting onto him.

TOM. What was he like?

MAGGIE. Very… normal. Learned that eccentrics are more my thing, only wish I'd known at the time. How about I sort out sleeping arrangements?

TOM. Sure.

MAGGIE. You don't mind staying?

TOM. No.

MAGGIE. Nice to have company for a change.

TOM. Know how you feel.

MAGGIE. Munchies big time – how about tea and toast in bed?

TOM. Sounds like a plan.

MAGGIE (*leaving*). Kettle's on the microwave. I'll throw a fresh cover on the duvet.

TOM *not sure what to do… goes into the kitchen.*

ADE *enters in semi-darkness.*

TOM *comes back carrying two mugs of tea.*

TOM. Jesus!

ADE. What you doing?

TOM. Frightened the life out of me, Ade, getting a cup of tea.

ADE. Two cups of tea.

TOM. Do you want one? Kettle's just boiled.

ADE. What you doing here?

TOM. Problem at work – bashed it out over a couple of pints.

ADE. Thought somebody was breaking in.

TOM. Me trashing your kitchen – too many sambucas.

ADE. Said you were drinking pints.

TOM. After the pints.

ADE. That's my dad's mug.

TOM. I didn't know.

ADE. Says 'World's Greatest Dad' on it.

TOM. Didn't see that.

ADE. In really big letters.

TOM. They are big, aren't they.

ADE. Bought it for Father's Day.

TOM. It's a great mug.

ADE. Crap present.

TOM. Be really chuffed if I got that off – my son. I don't, but if I did and he gave me that – I'd be really chuffed.

ADE. Where you sleeping?

TOM. Maggie… your mum's sorting me out now.

ADE. Thought we had an intruder – why I brought the knife.

TOM. Didn't see that.

ADE. Not got good night vision?

TOM. Would've really freaked me out.

ADE. No moon tonight. Things are different in the dark. Some things you see more clearly, other things just vanish. Big old wardrobe, during the day stands there like Big Ben, at night it's gone. But a little thing, like a glass, or a tiny ornament… that might stand out.

TOM. If it catches the light maybe?

ADE. Maybe.

TOM. Shall I put the knife back in the kitchen for you?

ADE. Keep it under the bed, new house, me and Mum on our own, can get creepy.

TOM. I'll take these up and come back. Fancy a quick game? Pwn some n00bs? Thought it was really funny what you said about me going camping.

ADE. Make my skin crawl – campers. Sneaking round, picking off easy targets.

TOM. We can't all have 'mad skillz' like you.

ADE. Is that what you think of Mum? Easy target?

TOM. No, no, God no.

ADE. Sit down, I'll tell you about my dad.

TOM *sits, sips his tea.*

He was a soldier.

TOM. I never knew that.

ADE. Bosnia, Kosovo – missed out this time round. Honourable discharge.

TOM. Your mum didn't tell me.

ADE. Part of the peacekeeping force, nasty, mass graves and all that. They stopped the Serbs killing the Albanians, then the Albanians started killing the Serbs. Ones that lived there peacefully all their lives – coz what the others had done. Think that's what did his head in.

TOM. The cycle of violence.

ADE. Made friends with these kids running a farm – lost their parents, cracking on with it themselves. Gang of twelve-, thirteen-year-olds, Serbs and Albanians together. Dad and his mates would get milk and cheese off them. Really good stuff, yogurt, goat cheese, everything.

TOM. Expect it was all organic too.

ADE. It was, it was delicious, he said it was.

TOM. Probably not pasteurised though – got to be careful with these foreign cheeses.

ADE. Turns up one day – half the kids burned on a haystack, charcoal skeletons, others all shot through the head. Coz they were working together.

TOM. That's…

ADE. Wasn't the same when he got back. Said they came to him in his dreams. Bodies hanging in basements. Two of his regiment killed by a tank mine.

TOM. Must be awful.

ADE. Mum couldn't cope, found a new boyfriend. Nice bloke – you remind me of him a bit. Dad found out and went psycho.

TOM. I didn't know.

ADE. Made a right mess of him. GBH – five years.

TOM. It's bound to have an effect.

ADE. Wouldn't have done that before. He'll be out soon.

TOM. Well, that's good news.

ADE. Called you a taxi.

TOM. If it's any consolation, Ade, there's technology being developed. To remove the soldier from the trauma of close combat.

ADE. Tell him yourself, when he gets back.

MAGGIE *enters*.

MAGGIE. What are you two doing in the dark?

TOM. Listen, Maggie – I'm going to shoot.

MAGGIE. Don't be silly, got the sofa bed out.

ADE *takes the knife into the kitchen*.

TOM. I've called a taxi.

MAGGIE (*calling through to* ADE). How come you have your friends stay over but I can't have mine?

TOM. Nothing to do with Ade – good night's sleep in my own bed.

MAGGIE. Much comfier than my bed, isn't it, Ade? Tell him how comfy the sofa bed is.

TOM. Think I understand why you're doing it – COLTIS. But I can't, you know, I just can't.

MAGGIE. Guess your holiday under tarpaulin is back on.

TOM. No – I'll rustle up a new pitch first thing. There's a juicy Eurorail contract out there somewhere.

MAGGIE. Take the holiday, Tom. You need it, we all do – taking a few days myself.

TOM. Thanks, Maggie, I'll do that. Had a great night.

MAGGIE. Me too.

1.9

Army Careers.
Worcester, UK.
Day 12.
09:07.

ADE *with a suitcase*.

NUGGET. Adrian – you've respawned.

ADE. Very good.

NUGGET. Who says I'm not down with the yutes. Off somewhere?

ADE. Come to sign up.

NUGGET. Been through all that – you failed the test.

ADE. Talked to Army Careers online – wasn't a proper test.

NUGGET. It was *my* proper test.

ADE. Wasn't the official entrance test.

NUGGET. It was the 'Entrance *to* the official entrance' test.

ADE. Said you got to process my application.

NUGGET. Not if you don't meet basic requirements.

ADE. For a different job. Definitely got the skills for this job.

NUGGET. What job?

ADE. UAV operator. They said you had to.

NUGGET. Better sit down then. What's in the suitcase?

ADE. Stuff for training camp.

NUGGET. You're hoping. UAV operator – what's that, RAF?

ADE. Royal Artillery – there's an advert on the website.

NUGGET (*reads*). 'A UAV is an unmanned spy plane with built-in camera to observe the battlefield. UAV operator controls the flight and interprets images to direct fire from guns and missiles onto targets.'

What do you want to do that for?

ADE. Reckon I'll be good at it.

NUGGET. Join the Army to point a camera on a glider?

ADE. Looks fun.

NUGGET. Watching telly all day except all that's on is sand? Every channel – sand. Ooh – there's a palm tree.

ADE. Looks good on the advert.

NUGGET. Course it does – be a crap advert otherwise.

ADE. Won't let me join as infantry.

NUGGET. Reckon you got the necessary skills?

ADE. Definitely – fly them using Xbox controllers.

NUGGET. Here we go.

ADE. It's on the advert, see for yourself.

NUGGET. They're not Xbox controllers.

ADE. Looks like them.

NUGGET. Might look like them – but they're not.

ADE. Exactly the same – without the Xbox logo.

NUGGET. Logo. No logo. Not the same.

ADE. Do it with my eyes closed.

NUGGET. I was escorting a relief convoy, get the paras out of Musa Qala. It's getting dark and two mullahs rock up pushing a rusty Volvo. We stop to let them cross, when the boot opens and out pops a granddad in a dress with an RPG. The rocket slams into the side of our Viking and all hell breaks – tracer fire from umpteen Taliban positions. We kick open the door just as another rocket hits – shrapnel rips across our driver's chest – one of his eyes is hanging out of its socket, his arms melted like candle wax down his uniform. We drag him through the firefight to the medic but an IED detonates and totals the ambulance. All we can do is take cover in the wreckage, stick our fists in his wounds to stop the blood.

These are not your usual flip-flop wearing useless bastards –
they're ex-mujahidin, hardened fighters. Through my night-
vision goggles I see foxes skulk out to feast on fresh meat.
They scatter when a truck pulls up with reinforcements, more
RPGs. I was whispering prayers, saying farewell to my
family. Just then we hear the rumble of a AC-130 gunship, it's
the Yanks but who cares – next thing the trees are a wall of
flame, the smell of burning flesh. Chinook came in and
airlifted the casualty back to base... he made it. That's no
UAV did that. That was real soldiers, real pilots, fighting to
save each other's lives.

ADE. What's your point?

NUGGET. Do something more useful.

ADE. Don't get more useful than UAVs. Reaper drones over
Afghanistan – blow up terrorists like that – (*Twitches his
finger.*) Fly them from a bunker in Las Vegas.

NUGGET. Been watching too much *Star Wars*, lad.

ADE. Drive to work, pwn a load of insurgents, pick up the kids,
go play the fruit machines.

NUGGET. Why don't you do that then?

ADE. Air Force, innit – camping n00bs.

NUGGET. Got a point there. Why not train as an engineer?
Eighty per cent of our jobs is non-combat. Postie? Still get the
uniform. Can you cook? Turn you into the next Jamie Oliver.

ADE. Would I need to go on the simulators?

NUGGET. You're like a toy with a string through its neck.

ADE. Lines get broken, firefight in the canteen – could happen.

NUGGET. We don't give guns to chefs – that's asking for
trouble.

ADE. They said you got to process my application.

NUGGET (*reads*). 'UAV operator is required to transport the
vehicle through hostile territory and may be required to
engage enemy forces.'

As previous – you don't have the necessary for combat personnel.

ADE. Said you got to online – and stop watching telly at work and fast-track me onto the simulators.

NUGGET. Who said?

ADE. Sergeant somebody.

NUGGET. Why didn't you say? Sergeant Somebody – know him well, old pal of mine. Do a deal with you, Adrian – tell me why you're so desperate for the simulators, and I'll personally arrange for you to go on them.

ADE. Want to join the Army.

NUGGET. And?

ADE. Want to know what it's like – so I'm one hunded per cent.

NUGGET. And?

ADE. There's this new game coming out, same programmers design your simulators.

NUGGET. Go on.

ADE. If I go on the simulators and I'm not one hundred per cent, then at least I'll totally pwn the game when it comes out and be able to join a professional clan.

NUGGET. Professional what?

ADE. Clan – team of players.

NUGGET. So basically – you been wasting my time.

ADE. We got a deal.

NUGGET. Got a memo through this morning – big thing going up in Brum. The 'Interactive Army Experience'. Simulators, consoles, careers advice – book you in soon as it opens.

ADE. When's that?

NUGGET. Next month some time.

ADE. The game comes out Monday.

NUGGET. Sorry, son – best I can do.

ADE. Wasting *your* time? Wasting my frakking time. Want your eyes tested, mate – do I look like pikey cannon fodder? Think I really wanted to be a minimum-wage murderer? Some brainless grunt with a gun?

NUGGET. No, Adrian, I didn't. Didn't think that for one moment.

2.1

Malvern Technology Centre.
Day 15.
11:27.

TOM *looks shook.*

MAGGIE. Not a good time, Tom.

TOM. Haven't been able to get hold of you.

MAGGIE. Back Wednesday – can we leave it till then?

TOM. Been down the lab – half the equipment's gone.

MAGGIE. Didn't you get the e-mail?

TOM. What e-mail?

MAGGIE. Forgot to click the mouse. (*She clicks.*) Going to
  Nevada for a couple of days.

TOM. Sounds nice, short break, shotgun wedding in Las Vegas?

MAGGIE. Everyone is creaming about the work, you should be
  really proud.

TOM. I'm all puffed up – people breaking into the lab, stealing
  my laser radar.

MAGGIE. It's not yours, Tom, they found a buyer for their
  product.

TOM. Thought we were taking a holiday – not doing trials then
  sneaking off to Nevada.

MAGGIE. We got a call from Whitehall – what was I supposed
  to do?

TOM. Tell them it's for civil applications – always has been.

MAGGIE. They want us to pitch for FCS.

TOM. FCS?

MAGGIE. Future Combat Systems.

TOM. I know what FCS stands for. You said this was for our boys – no more coffins in Union Jacks.

MAGGIE. They invited a few suits from Washington.

TOM. Half the bloody Pentagon was there – like walking onto the bridge of the *Starship Enterprise*.

MAGGIE. Your *Star Trek* quips didn't go unnoticed. You weren't supposed to be there, Tom.

TOM. At the trial of my own radar?

MAGGIE. It isn't yours – what do you think your salary is for?

TOM. One minute COLTIS is to develop the rail network, next it's targeting for the MoD – that's bad enough, but not the bloody Americans.

MAGGIE. What have you got against the Americans?

TOM. Where to begin? How about the most progressive foreign policy since the Third Reich?

MAGGIE. That's all changed now.

TOM. Got the games console in your office.

MAGGIE. Any aggro from a customer – I can pwn some n00bs.

TOM. Feeling a bit of a n00b myself.

MAGGIE. Sorry, Tom – I had no choice.

TOM. And the two dudes with the gamepads?

MAGGIE. What two dudes?

TOM. Two Marines testing COLTIS, what's with operating the radar with PlayStation controllers…

MAGGIE. They weren't PlayStation…

TOM. Potentially weaponised UAVs, targeting, using Xbox controllers…

MAGGIE. It wasn't Xbox…

TOM. Gamepads – all the same.

MAGGIE. They were probably just messing around.

TOM. That's what I'm worried about.

MAGGIE. It's programmed to network with the Army OS – the machine-human interface is arbitrary.

TOM. Plug and play! Stick a gamepad in the USB and pwn a few Arabs – real ones.

MAGGIE. Gamepads won't exist in a couple of years – it'll be motion sensors, neuroscanners.

TOM. Clued-up on gaming technology of a sudden.

MAGGIE. We're selling this to the Americans on usability – the platform needs to be flexible.

TOM. See where this is going – a giant amusement arcade in the middle of the desert! Better still, kids can fly missions direct from their bedroom.

MAGGIE. Grow up, Tom – the technology is universal. Like saying you can't put wheels on tanks because kids have bikes.

TOM. Tanks don't have wheels – they're caterpillar tracks.

MAGGIE. There are wheels inside the caterpillar tracks.

TOM. Those aren't wheels – they're rollers.

MAGGIE. What the hell is a roller if it isn't a wheel?

TOM. Completely different. And what meathead called the thing a Weaponised Microdrone? Catchy acronym – WMD.

MAGGIE. We're branding it WepMD.

TOM. Well, that'll fool 'em! Did they teach that on your MBA? There's me thinking bogus qualification, corporate bullshit, turns out you're radical thinkers, paradigm shifters – WepMD! Fucking genius!

MAGGIE. We are at war, Tom, whatever we can do to help our troops, to get them out alive.

TOM. Gone too far this time – I won't do it.

MAGGIE. Not asking you to do it – I'm going to pitch.

TOM. Won't be much of a pitch without a live demo.

MAGGIE. We're taking Rob and Graham – they can tech this.

TOM. They'll say no, they're my team.

MAGGIE. Who do you think set up COLTIS for the trial?

TOM. Did you ask them? Did they do it?

MAGGIE. Sorry, Tom – I know this is difficult for you. It's best for everyone if you take a step back, have a couple of weeks, finish your camping holiday.

TOM. I'm not camping – that's your unhinged son, taking the piss.

MAGGIE. What do you mean?

TOM. The game – saying I'm a coward.

MAGGIE. Why do you say unhinged?

TOM. Do sane kids pull knives on their guests?

MAGGIE. Are you serious?

TOM. Very.

MAGGIE. What happened? Why didn't you say anything?

TOM. Obviously had a rough time with his dad.

MAGGIE. He threatened you, with a knife?

TOM. Wasn't that bad – not like being mugged by my workmates.

MAGGIE*'s phone rings.*

MAGGIE. Sorry, Tom – I have to take this call.

David – any news?

Have you checked the airport?

No, nothing.

Got a car waiting, my flight leaves in two hours.

Call me back if you hear anything.

TOM. Ade's dad? Not in prison then.

MAGGIE. Could be, he's a defence barrister, not a particularly good one – where most of his clients end up.

TOM. Did you put him up to that? The 'fucked-up dad in Kosovo' monologue?

MAGGIE. Is that what he told you?

TOM. Pretty lethal mother-son combo going there – I nearly agreed to do it, you know, the trial.

MAGGIE. He's packed a suitcase, been gone since Friday.

TOM. You can't do this, Maggie – it's my baby, said so yourself. If Rob and Graham get a tech question they can't answer, we'll look like amateurs. I know every millimetre of silicon...

MAGGIE *cries*.

I'm sure he'll turn up. If there's anything I can do.

2.2

ADE *in camos and face paint*.

Opens his suitcase, takes out a 'pop-up' tent, pops it up.

Pulls out a crate of Red Bull, opens one, drinks.

2.3

Army Careers.
Worcester, UK.
Day 15.
16:08.

The news on TV in background.

MAGGIE. Found a magazine under his bed.

NUGGET. Fairly normal for a teenage lad.

MAGGIE. One of your magazines.

NUGGET. I know – what did you think I meant?

MAGGIE. He's gone missing.

NUGGET. Take a look on the computer.

MAGGIE. Never shown any interest in that sort of thing.

NUGGET. What sort of thing?

MAGGIE. The Army sort of thing.

TOM. Probably lost in a book somewhere, reading Plato, or gaming.

NUGGET. Plato?

MAGGIE. He's going to uni, wants to study Classics.

NUGGET. Ancient Greek, pwns n00bs?

MAGGIE. n00bs?

NUGGET. Total ignorants, he taught me that.

MAGGIE. Adrian's been in here?

NUGGET. Nice lad – video games and Greek.

MAGGIE. What did he want?

NUGGET. Good question.

MAGGIE. He's seventeen, he's going to university.

TOM. Doesn't sound like he signed up or anything stupid.

MAGGIE. Did you give him that magazine?

NUGGET. Like your husband says – no damage done.

MAGGIE. Squaddies in the gym, parades, white-water rafting…

TOM. No, I'm…

MAGGIE. No, Tom – they're like a cult, preying on confused kids.

TOM. I'm…

MAGGIE. Peddle my son that filth and he goes missing and you call that no damage…

NUGGET. Nothing on the computer.

MAGGIE. Bet he's just the fresh meat you're looking for.

NUGGET. Most lads come in with friends or family in the forces, know what it's like from inside. Get a lot of professionals – fed up with the hamster wheel. Kids surrounded by drugs and crime, think the Army's a better choice, wouldn't argue with that. I'll stick my head in the office, see if anyone knows anything.

He goes into the office.

A REPORTER *on TV, subtitles:*

Hundreds of fans are queuing to get their hands on Modern War: Future Warrior – latest instalment of the controversial war game.

MAGGIE. Sorry.

TOM. That's okay.

Adrian, how long have you been here?

MAGGIE. Didn't think it would help him knowing we weren't.

TOM. Sure.

About 38 hours.

MAGGIE. You don't mind?

Long time to queue for a computer game?

TOM. No, I don't mind. Guess that makes me Mr Cole.

There's a tank driving up and down giving out energy drinks, so it's been okay.

MAGGIE. What's he thinking of?

What is it about this game that's so special?

NUGGET *returns with a form.*

NUGGET. As mentioned, Adrian came in on the 12th, discussed various opportunities, no sign since. Seemed very interested in the simulators. If there's serious concerns, we'll contact emergency services, send a description to missing persons.

Designed by the same team as the Army simulators, plus all the latest military tech.

TOM. Could you turn up the TV?

On TV:

REPORTER. In the last game you had to kill shoppers in Oxford Street – will this feature similar shocking material?

ADE. Didn't have to shoot the civilians – you could, but you didn't have to.

REPORTER. What did you do – when you played that level?

ADE. I killed them. Few dozen shoppers, or the nuke goes, then it's millions.

REPORTER. You'll be the first person to get your hands on the new game – what will you do then?

ADE. Pwn it.

REPORTER. Yes, I suppose you would. Thanks, Adrian – seven hours, fifty-two minutes and counting.

Crowd cheers.

ADE (*over them*). I'm turning pro-gamer, professional clans look out for me on the leaderboard – n00bassassin93.

NUGGET. Leave you to savour the family reunion.

NUGGET *goes.*

MAGGIE. Why is Ade on the news?

TOM. Queuing for the new game – Future Warrior.

MAGGIE. In uniform?

TOM. Hardcore fans get dressed up.

MAGGIE. In a strange place between utter relief and absolute fury.

TOM. He's not going anywhere – released at midnight.

MAGGIE. This has gone too far – I'm going to get him.

TOM. What about FCS?

MAGGIE. I'll have to cancel. Put back the pitch.

TOM. Can you afford to do that?

MAGGIE. Absolutely not – the department depends on it.

TOM. There are two of us, Mrs Cole – if Mr Cole can help in any way?

MAGGIE. No.

TOM. Why not?

MAGGIE. You don't want COLTIS to go military.

TOM. I will not bomb the pitch.

MAGGIE. You're not pitching, Tom – all know how you feel about this.

TOM. If it's going ahead anyway…

MAGGIE. Our jobs, everything we've worked for.

TOM. Make sure they do it properly – no gamepads.

MAGGIE. You don't understand, you haven't got a family.

TOM. I know the product better than anyone – I created it.

MAGGIE. My home, the education of my son.

TOM. Breathed life into it, my life, best part of a decade – can't just hand it over and forget about it.

MAGGIE. No – this is too important.

TOM. You have to let me do it, Maggie. Rob and Graham won't be able to recalibrate the optical amplifier. English countryside, Nevada desert – completely different atmospheric conditions, play havoc with the imaging – false targets, potentially lethal. I've got the blueprints of every circuit burned in my mind...

MAGGIE. No, Tom.

TOM. I swear I will not sabotage the pitch, I understand how much this means to you – because it means even more to me.

MAGGIE *glances at the TV.*

I swear to you, on my mother's life, I swear to you.

MAGGIE. On your mother's life?

TOM. Yes.

MAGGIE. You swear you will pitch to the very best of your ability, on your mother's life.

TOM. I do. I swear.

MAGGIE. Is she still alive?

TOM. And kicking – very much so.

2.4

Clock counts down.

23:59:45.
23:59:46.
23:59:47.

On TV:

REPORTER. Looks like they're about to open the doors.

CROWD. Ten, nine, eight, seven, six, five, four, three, two, one...

00:00.
Modern War: Future Warrior.

GENERAL JONES – *in upgraded uniform*.

GENERAL JONES. We are the most powerful force in the history of man. Every war is our war, because what happens over there, matters over here. Learning to use the tools of modern warfare, is the difference between prosperity and utter destruction. Same shit, different enemy, new toys.

ADE hunched over a gamepad, swigs from a Red Bull, a crate at his feet.

Yesterday you were a soldier on the front line – but today front lines are history. Our enemies have fled the battlefield – the hostiles are amongst us and war rages everywhere.

Press X to play multiplayer online.

ADE. Bring it on, n00bs.

GENERAL JONES. Multiplayer Team Deathmatch – let's do this.

Press P to pick up modular assault rifle.

Machine-gun fire – scream of a dying man.

You killed NakedSnake38.

Use killstreaks to unlock military technology. Frag out.

Grenade explodes – scream of a dying man.

You killed ZombieNosh.

MAGGIE (*shouts up*). Ade? Anybody home?

GENERAL JONES. Hostiles ahead. Move quickly.

Sustained machine-gun fire – screams of dying men.

MAGGIE. Been to Oxford Street, and back, nice to come and say hello, if you're here…

5 KILLSTREAK.
Press R2 for robotic sentry gun.

ADE. Be rude not to.

MAGGIE. And I'm hoping you are.

GENERAL JONES. Robotic sentry gun online.

Intense heavy gunfire.

You killed butang2.
You killed CrayzeePaul.
You killed mrZeppelin.
You killed TotallyNumb.

You've been promoted – Private First Class!

Private First Class.

ADE (*putting his headset on*). This is n00bassassin live – totally pwning Future Warrior…

MAGGIE. Ade – it's me, are you in there?

ADE. Another uber-sick sequel, loving the new tech on the killstreaks.

MAGGIE. Going AWOL, threatening Tom, hanging around Army Careers, on TV dressed as a soldier…

ADE. Any pro-clans, I'm nudging top 10K, KDR 9.7, here all night.

MAGGIE. Just a friendly chat, really. Going to try the door now – don't be angry, I have asked.

Intense gunfire from robotic sentry gun.

USAF base.
Nevada, USA.

TOM. Ladies and gentlemen – it's a great honour to be here today. Three hundred years ago the musketeer replaced the archer – and as firearms retired bows and arrows in the eighteenth century, the weaponised microdrone or WepMD will retire the soldier's rifle in the twenty-first.

GENERAL JONES. Picking up movement on the thermal radar.

TOM. The eyes and ears of this revolution are COLTIS. Thermal imagers locate hidden targets, and 3D laser radar makes detailed target assessment – from an AK-47 to a Scud missile.

GENERAL JONES. Frag out.

Grenade explodes – screams of dying men.

TOM. Payloads are then tailored for the remote soldier to deploy.

GENERAL JONES. Triple kill – you'll be decorated for this, soldier.

TOM. WepMD is specifically designed for urban, asymmetric conflict. This state-of-the-art technology replaces the rifle as our primary weapon, and reduces risk to life and limb by removing our troops from close combat.

GENERAL JONES. Don't forget Iron Age technology for close combat.

Press R3 to attack with melee weapon.

TOM. COLTIS is so precise it can identify a kitchen knife at five miles.

Slits a throat – choking of a dying man.

You killed evilbeard3D.

So no problems getting back to the mess tent.

10 KILLSTREAK.
Press R2 for Predator drone.

ADE. In n00bassassin we trust.

GENERAL JONES. Predator drone online, smart bomb ready for launch.

TOM. Joking aside, we've all witnessed the unmanned revolution in the air – now it's time for ground troops to get their Predator drone.

A massive explosion.

Omnicide bonus – you killed the entire enemy team!

Today heralds a new era in modern warfare. The horror we read about every day will at last be consigned to history books. Now, let's make our way to the strip where General Jones is flying in for the live demo.

A helicopter swoops overhead.

GENERAL JONES. You've been promoted – Lance Corporal!

Lance Corporal.

You've been promoted – Staff Sergeant!

Staff Sergeant.

You've been promoted – Second Lieutenant!

Second Lieutenant.
Time played: 6 hours 17 mins.
Leaderboard ranking: 2872.

Half the Red Bulls drunk.

Outgunned and outnumbered – but with the tools of modern warfare at our fingertips. Enemy Cobra inbound.

Gatling-gun fire from helicopter.

ADE. Try to n00btube me?

Press L1 to aim Stinger missile.

GENERAL JONES. Locking on target.

ADE. Taste of your own…

The missile hits, explodes, helicopter crashes.

You killed YuteKilla59.

GENERAL JONES. You fried 'em. Enemy respawn portal located.

ADE. Not camping – just passing through…'

MAGGIE. I'm camped here till you come out or come home, Ade.

ADE. Needing another killstreak.

GENERAL JONES. Frag out.

Grenade explodes – scream of a dying man.

You killed ZombieNosh.

TOM. If you look down the strip, WepMD is about to make her first hover-by. A ruggedised weapons controller is in development, but for today's demo, I borrowed my son's.

He takes a gamepad from his bag, presses a button.

MAGGIE. You're not in trouble – I'm just worried about you.

WepMD27i online.

TOM. WepMD is powered by an Ardour 27i Rolls Royce engine. It comes with four mini-Hellfire missiles, two 10mm Vulcan cannons and a point five calibre Gatling gun.

Machine-gun fire – screams of dying men.

Press A to activate COLTIS targeting.

But COLTIS is the brain behind the brawn.

GENERAL JONES. Hostiles ahead – move quickly.

Target identified – low-grade armour, AK-47.

TOM. COLTIS is so precise, identifying targets in such detail, it removes all possibility of human error.

Machine-gun fire – scream of a dying man.

GENERAL JONES. Target neutralised.

TOM. Once we lock on – you can toggle between weapons.

Press C to cycle payloads.

MAGGIE. Not a minute goes by I don't think of you, Ade.

TOM. Now we get to see if WepMD walks the walk.

GENERAL JONES. Use killstreaks to unlock military technology.

MAGGIE. I'd forgive you anything, Adrian Cole.

TOM. So first offering payloads…

Mini-Hellfire missile x4.
10mm Vulcan cannon.
Snickers bar.

MAGGIE. No job, no man, no argument could ever come between us.

TOM. Then selecting our weapon of choice.

Snickers bar selected.

And deploy.

Press R1 to unwrap the weapon.

MAGGIE. You're hard-wired into my heart.

TOM. Now, when it says unwrap – that's an English colloquialism. But what we're really focusing on today is targeting capability.

Machine-gun fire – scream of a dying man.

GENERAL JONES. Target neutralised.

MAGGIE. Remember the stories we used to read?

TOM. Simply toggle between hostiles.

MAGGIE. *Jason and the Argonauts*, *The Golden Fleece*.

Target identified – politically unstable, oil/mineral rich nations.

TOM. Then choose how to engage the evil-doers.

Press R3 to enter into peace negotiations.

Bit formal, bit stiff that one maybe. How about...

Press L2 to invite the enemy over for a nice cup of tea.

I guess coffee is more your thing. Sorry, Mum.

MAGGIE. Monsters were your favourite – the Cyclops, seven-headed Hydra, Medusa...

GENERAL JONES. Picking up movement on the thermal.

TOM. Talking to one of your officers earlier, he said 'Sir' – which you all say with alarming regularity...

Machine-gun fire – scream of a dying man.

Sure you mean well, but just seems disingenuous...

MAGGIE. Always looked her straight in the eye...

TOM. Try an online dictionary – 'Sir' he said – 'the great thing about robots is...

GENERAL JONES. Frag out.

MAGGIE. You were never afraid...

Grenade explodes – screams of dying men.

TOM.... when they get shot, you don't have to send a letter home to their parents.'

GENERAL JONES. Quadruple kill.

MAGGIE. So small, so fearless…

GENERAL JONES. You'll be decorated for this, soldier.

TOM. But I just…

MAGGIE. I just want you to know…

TOM.... think it's important you know…

MAGGIE.... that you're everything to me…

TOM.... that this technology is…

Slits a throat – choking of a dying man.

MAGGIE.... the only achievement in my life.

TOM.... WepMD, COLTIS is…

MAGGIE. The only thing that really matters to me.

Machine-gun fire – screams of dying men.

TOM.... is… is… is…

GENERAL JONES. Target neutralised.

TOM. I'm terribly sorry… I… Could you please excuse me…

25 KILLSTREAK.
Press R2 to launch WepMD.

GENERAL JONES. WepMD online. Designate targets for remote attack.

Ground-shaking throb of deep explosions.

You killed FallenAngel76.
You killed AlphaSAA.
You killed ZombieNosh.
You killed senior-frito911.
You killed iRambo.
You killed KlownSnypr.

ADE *screams with delight.*

Sand and rocks, stained with a thousand years of blood, will never forget this.

MAGGIE. Ade? Are you in there?

ADE. FRAKKING KILLSTREAK DUDE!

GENERAL JONES. Experts in the science of violence.

MAGGIE. ADRIAN! OPEN THIS DOOR AT ONCE!

The pwnage continues.

GENERAL JONES. You've been promoted – First Lieutenant!

First Lieutenant.

You've been promoted – Captain!

Captain.

You've been promoted – Brigadier General!

Brigadier General.
Time played: 17 hours 22 minutes.
Leaderboard ranking: 154.

All the Red Bulls drunk.

TOM *appears with gamepad, a half-drunk bottle of whiskey.*

TOM. Console in my hotel. Uber-cool is that? Console in my hotel room? It's an X…

GENERAL JONES. We advance like breath exhaled from the earth…

TOM. PSbox – 3 – 3 – XPS60…

GENERAL JONES. With progress – we will prevail.

TOM. Pestbox 360.

ADE *urinates into an empty Red Bull can.*

ZombieNosh wants to be your friend.

ADE. Nosh on this, zombie man.

TOM. It's a Pestbox!

BadMuvva68 has joined the game.

MAGGIE *reappears, hunched over a gamepad.*

MAGGIE. Hi, Ade.

ADE. Mum! How you get in?

MAGGIE. On the console downstairs.

ADE. Not now, Mum – I'm on a killstreak.

MAGGIE. Been outside your door for hours.

ADE. On a killstreak.

MAGGIE. Seven hours.

ADE. Epic killstreak.

GENERAL JONES. Vulcan cannon selected.

MAGGIE. Had to go out and buy the game.

ADE. Awesome, dude, or what?

MAGGIE. We need to talk, Ade.

Cannon fire – screams of dying men.

GENERAL JONES. You've been promoted – Lieutenant General!

Lieutenant General.

ADE. No, Mum – totally pwning the leaderboards. Taking off my headset, this is too important.

MAGGIE. Don't you dare, Adrian.

ADE *takes off his headset.*

TomTheTommy has joined the game.

Tom – is that you?

TOM. Console in my hotel room.

MAGGIE. I need your help, Tom. Ade's locked in…

TOM. It's a Pestbox.

MAGGIE. Barricaded himself in his room.

TOM. Maggie, Maggie, Maggie – it's all good. I couldn't do it.

MAGGIE. You couldn't do the pitch?

TOM. No, I did it, no, I did it, no, all good, couldn't do it.

MAGGIE. What happened, Tom?

TOM. Don't worry, it's all good, she's going to kill me.

MAGGIE. What did you do? What did FCS say?

TOM. No news is good news.

MAGGIE. Are you drunk, Tom?

TOM. Just a couple of ales, officer... 'This is the No News from
the BBC'... tell the truth... absolutely shat-faced... they did
it... your lot...

MAGGIE. Rob and Graham did the demo?

TOM. I don't know, think so, I just...

MAGGIE. Forget about that for now – I need your help.

TOM. Tried to kill it... couldn't... sorry, Mum.

MAGGIE. Ade's locked himself in his room, playing the game.

TOM. Get him on the Pestbox.

MAGGIE. How do you play this one?

TOM. Same – new stuff on the killstreaks. I miss you, Maggie.

MAGGIE. Miss you too, Tom. What do I do?

Press X to play multiplayer online.

TOM. Press X.

GENERAL JONES. Multiplayer Team Deathmatch – let's do
this!

Cannon fire, rockets, apocalypse.

You killed Not-Charlie-B.
You killed FeaRMoho.
You killed butang2.
You killed teh_pwnerer.

ADE. Sickest killstreak ever, dude.

You killed Xcluvs1v3.
You killed SnappyGabardini.
You killed sLIPunisher.
You killed KingRollo.

TOM. Sounds like some serious beef – stay in cover.

You killed N2D S4V4GE.
You killed ZombieNosh.
Double Omnicide bonus!

GENERAL JONES. You've been promoted – Commander-in-chief!

Commander-in-chief.

ADE. EPIC. FRAKKING. UBER. PWNAGE!!!

The pwnage continues.

MAGGIE. Where is he?

TOM. Hunched over a laptop somewhere – flying his killstreak.

GENERAL JONES. You've been promoted – Commander-in-chief!

Commander-in-chief.
Leaderboard ranking: 1st.

ADE. This is, this is…

MAGGIE. Where are we going?

TOM. There's a little bunker I know, candlelight and fine wine, bazooka at every table.

GENERAL JONES. You've been promoted – Commander-in-chief!

Commander-in-chief.
Leaderboard ranking: 1st

MAGGIE. What did you say?

ADE. This is, this is…

GENERAL JONES. You've been promoted – Commander-in-chief!

Commander-in-chief.
Leaderboard ranking: 1st.

ADE. This is, this is… *camping*. Frakking *camping*, dude.

TOM. Stay close – sounds like uber-pwnage.

ADE. Future Warrior? Future *Camper* more like – n00biest frakking *camping* I ever saw.

MAGGIE. Can't hear you, Tom.

ADE. I'm a God. A *camping* God – tech turned me into the campest n00by uber-camper in the history of camping.

TOM. Picking up something on my thermal radar.

ADE. IT'S FRAKKING CAMPING, DUDES!!!!

A SOLDIER *smashes through the door in full special-ops gear, gas mask and sub-machine gun.*

The SOLDIER *stands breathing, inert, waiting for the next command.*

MAGGIE. Is that him?

TOM. n00bassassin93.

MAGGIE. Like a little boy, playing a computer game.

TOM. Flying his revolutionary technology. Go on.

MAGGIE. Sneak up from behind?

TOM. Never beat him face to face.

MAGGIE. Doesn't seem right.

TOM. We don't have any choice.

Press R3 to attack with melee weapon.

The SOLDIER *pulls a huge knife…*

Pwn him.

MAGGIE. Sorry, Ade.

The SOLDIER *slits* ADE's *throat.*

He collapses in a pool of blood.

n00bassassin93 KIA.
Respawn in 5.
4.
3.
2.
1.
0.

The game is switched off.

2.5

Worcester Royal Hospital.
Day 20.
14:21.

MAGGIE *outside* ADE*'s room.*

TOM *with a plastic bag.*

TOM. Hey.

MAGGIE. No need for you to come.

TOM. How's he doing?

MAGGIE. Keeping him in a few days – observation. He'll be fine.

TOM. What's the prognosis?

MAGGIE. Exhaustion, lack of sleep…

TOM. Seventeen hours – bender by any standards.

MAGGIE. And five hundred milligrams of caffeine in his blood.

TOM. That would do it. Brought Ade a card.

MAGGIE. One of those really big ones?

TOM. Picked something up in the States – everything so cheap. One of those motion sensors – play using body movements, aim, pull the trigger, no buttons, nothing.

MAGGIE. Bit inappropriate maybe.

TOM. Or car racing – no wheel required, doesn't have to be shooters.

MAGGIE. So – how was it?

TOM. Pleasantly surprised – all the horror stories about the locals.

MAGGIE. Love their scientists – they invented the nerd.

TOM. There was this dinner before the demo, never seen so much grilled flesh. Buffalo, wild boar – melted in your mouth like marshmallow.

MAGGIE. Hope you packed your digital meat thermometer.

TOM. Had their own in the kitchen.

MAGGIE. That's a boon.

TOM. They invited along some vets.

MAGGIE. Bit late for the buffalo and wild boar, wasn't it?

TOM. No, Marines, Special Forces. Messed up pretty bad – IEDs, suicide bombers. Greeted me like a hero, held me in their arms and cried. They were very drunk.

MAGGIE. Says the man on the Pestbox. Strictly off record – I'm glad you sabotaged the pitch. Seeing Ade in there, bit of a wake-up call. And I wanted to apologise, was a bit of a bully – you stood up for your principles.

TOM. Mine, my mum's... not really sure.

MAGGIE. Got a meet with the CEO tomorrow. Told them I made you cover, family emergency all that. Recommended a transfer, so you'd still have access to the research – they could give us both P45s.

TOM. Starting to think a change might be a good thing.

MAGGIE. You know they had WepMD in the game? One of the killstreaks, in the game before it's on the battlefield. Anyway, looks like the whole project is going into cold storage. Saw them packing up the lab yesterday – must have mixed feelings.

TOM. It's a buy-out.

MAGGIE. A fire sale? I'm sorry, Tom, scrap value can hardly be worth it.

TOM. Shipping to Nevada – FCS.

MAGGIE. They're buying COLTIS?

TOM. No. The whole department. COLTIS, the labs, your desk, Snickers bars in your desk...

MAGGIE. You bombed the pitch – I heard it was moronic and offensive.

TOM. That was the general idea – they thought it very Python-esque. Pretty surreal couple of days, actually – sobered up in a brothel downtown Vegas... girls like I have never...

MAGGIE. Tom?

TOM. Couple of flatheads from military intelligence turned up, paid the bill. Bizarre.

MAGGIE. According to legend it stays in Vegas – *if* you don't go telling everyone yourself.

TOM. The CEO will let you know tomorrow.

MAGGIE. Let me know what?

TOM. Offering excellent terms – voluntary redundancy, understand some of us won't want to go.

MAGGIE. How do you know all this?

TOM. I got a call. They suggested the novel idea scientists might be capable of managing themselves.

MAGGIE. Am I being fired?

TOM. No – don't be silly. They've asked me to install a data-link in COLTIS, everything streamed back to base, stored, analysed – soldiers will be accountable for every bullet they fire.

MAGGIE. You're going to do it?

TOM. There's a real sense of idealism there – President with the Nobel Peace Prize. All kinds of safety processes we need to incorporate. Establish best practice from the top down.

MAGGIE. Best practice? They're giving you my job?

TOM. Creative control over COLTIS, it's not about jobs.

MAGGIE. You never wanted this, Tom.

TOM. My mother never wanted this. I don't agree with it but somebody has to take responsibility how this is applied. The buck stops here.

MAGGIE. Sounds like the buck's stopped in your pocket.

TOM. You're very welcome on board – we'll be needing an office manager.

MAGGIE. Office manager? Not my thing – pretty handy with a mop and bucket, though.

TOM. No need to be like that, Maggie.

MAGGIE. I'll take my chances with the CEO, need to do a rejig of priorities myself.

TOM. The universities are amazing – FCS pay college fees for dependents. University of Nevada, I checked online, top-rated Ancient History department.

MAGGIE. Thanks, Tom – not the best time to pick up sticks.

TOM. Made up my mind – it's the only thing to do. Realise it must be a bit of a blow.

MAGGIE. Don't worry – we'll soldier on.

TOM. I know you were keen... but... I've got my baby back and she's going to need all my attention.

MAGGIE. What do you mean?

TOM. COLTIS.

MAGGIE. The stuff about being keen?

TOM. Come on, Maggie – it's a machine, you can't be jealous. I woke up, smelled the coffee, realised how important the smell of coffee is to me.

MAGGIE. What are you talking about, Tom?

TOM. COLTIS – it's my life. Couldn't sacrifice that for anyone – not even you.

MAGGIE. This gets better and better!

TOM. Bit of a double-whammy, I know. Stay with friends, keep busy.

MAGGIE *laughs*.

Whatever you need to do.

She laughs harder.

Give it time, be gentle on yourself, nothing you could do to make me change my mind.

MAGGIE. That's good advice.

TOM. Call me if you like… maybe that's a bad idea… but I'm always there, if you needed a friend.

MAGGIE *tries to stifle her laughter.*

You're crying a bit.

MAGGIE. Yes, yes… I am.

TOM. Still like Ade to come visit – if that's not too awkward.

MAGGIE. No. I mean yes – obviously it could be. Fine, Tom.

TOM. The offer about uni was genuine. If he wants to study there, and it's a bloody good idea, I could pull some strings.

MAGGIE. Very generous, under the circumstances.

TOM. Part of the reason I wanted to see him. There's a bursary programme – want to have a chat with him about it.

MAGGIE. Bursary programme?

TOM. FCS is keen on getting young minds involved, so they set up this bursary scheme with the uni.

MAGGIE. What kind of scheme?

TOM. Enrolling a group of youngsters for beta testing. Want to see what happens when alternative skill-sets are brought to the technology.

MAGGIE. You mean gamers?

TOM. People who demonstrate a natural affinity for the micromanagement aspects of WepMD.

MAGGIE. You mean gamers.

TOM. Those who possess the appropriate aptitudes.

MAGGIE. Gamers.

TOM. Civil applications too – coastguard, traffic police, border control, all phasing-in UAVs. We've rented a small mountain range in Haiti, how cool is that, our own mountain range to play on?

MAGGIE. You want to take Ade to Haiti to fly WepMD?

TOM. No. The control centre is in Nevada, like the drones – but ground units.

MAGGIE. Get out, Tom.

TOM. You're upset, have a ponder when you've calmed down.

MAGGIE. I don't need a ponder.

TOM. Say hello to Ade and then I'll be off.

MAGGIE. Don't you go anywhere near my son with that.

TOM. They're in the shops – can buy them anywhere.

MAGGIE. Get out – take it with you.

TOM. Just give him the card then.

MAGGIE. I'll give that to him.

He hands MAGGIE *the card.*

What's inside?

TOM. Nothing. A card.

MAGGIE. What have you written inside?

TOM. Get well soon – words to that effect.

MAGGIE. Your contact details?

TOM. I think Ade is old enough to decide for himself…

MAGGIE *rips the card into small pieces – sprinkles it in front of* ADE's *door.*

TOM *steps back.*

Really enjoyed working with you, Maggie. Sorry things didn't work out.

2.6

Army Careers.
Worcester, UK.
Day 30.
15:48.

NUGGET. We're closing – four o'clock Fridays.

ADE. I was in the other week.

NUGGET. Adrian – respawned again, must be a portal nearby.

ADE. Brought back the magazine.

NUGGET. Wasn't expecting to see you again.

ADE. I wanted to…

NUGGET. Don't tell me – you want to go on the simulators.

ADE. No.

NUGGET. Course, no need – you pwn the game now. Saw you on the news.

ADE. Embarrassing.

NUGGET. What can this minimum-wage murderer do for you?

ADE. I wanted to – came to say sorry. Had time to think about stuff.

NUGGET. What stuff?

ADE. The games, simulators, then I started to think about Plato.

NUGGET. You started to think about Plato – made you come in to apologise. How does that work?

ADE. I don't know. Had interview for uni today.

NUGGET. How did it go?

ADE. I went off on one. Told them all about it – Plato and computer games. He's got this idea, 'Theory of Forms', you know it?

NUGGET. Pikey cannon fodder? Grunt with a gun like me?

ADE. Sorry, I was bang out of order.

NUGGET. As a matter of fact – I don't.

ADE. He reckons everything is a bad copy of its perfect form. Says it's like we're in a cave, looking at shadows on the wall, but the ideas themselves, true reality, that's outside and we can never see it. My Greek teacher says it's bollocks, but I reckon he was on to something. Wasn't describing life as it is – he was predicting the future.

NUGGET. I think you'll be going to uni.

ADE. But these shadows aren't like normal shadows. They're opposite – brighter and more colourful than reality. Games, simulators, UAVs – beautiful, like the Sirens, irresistible. This is only the beginning. Won't be no humans, not on our side. Last chance to know what the Greeks were banging on about.

NUGGET. Not sure I follow – but sounds very interesting.

ADE. I want to sign up.

NUGGET. Here we go…

ADE. I mean it this time.

NUGGET. Course you do, son.

ADE. Got to be a soldier – before it's too late.

NUGGET. Not signing you up so you can go on the simulators.

ADE. Not listening – last thing I want to do.

NUGGET. You failed the tests – all of them. Disrespectful to a superior, bloody rude.

ADE. The US Air Force recruits more remote pilots than real ones now – fact.

NUGGET. Playing too much Space Invaders, lad.

ADE. Makes us look like the bad guys – *Death Star*, Terminators, the humans are the Rebel Alliance, we're the Evil Empire.

NUGGET. You want to join the Army so we don't look like the bad guys?

ADE. I got to know what it is – before it's all shadows on screens.

NUGGET. Sounds to me like you been on the wacky baccy.

ADE. Stopped all that.

NUGGET. So you have been on the wacky baccy?

ADE. Not any more. Joined a gym, ran fifteen miles last week.

NUGGET. Stand up.

ADE *stands*.

Seen more meat on a string of cheese.

ADE. Please, got to do this, whatever it takes, train twenty-four-seven, don't care how long, one thing in my mind, sign up, nothing else matters.

NUGGET. I can't sign you, Adrian.

ADE. I'm ready, mentally, you want to test me, I'll take you on, I'm ready for it.

NUGGET. Even if you beefed up, even if you were ready – I'm back on civvy street, officially retired as of two minutes ago.

ADE. Why you retiring?

NUGGET. Long story. Not been hitting my targets.

ADE. That's funny.

NUGGET. What is?

ADE. Soldier not hitting his targets.

NUGGET. They offered me a new job – up in Brum, at the Interactive Army Experience.

ADE. The simulators?

NUGGET. Asked me to be a 'facilitator'. Give the kids background info on the... rides, I nearly called 'em. Crowd control.

ADE. You don't want to?

NUGGET. Too old for that cabaret. Like to spend more time in the garden.

ADE. Gardens are good.

NUGGET. Don't actually have a garden – whacked a load of crazy paving over it soon as we moved in, but I'm going to get that up, start a vegetable patch. Carrots, potatoes, tomatoes – nothing fancy. I hear runner beans grow quickly and they have a lovely red blossom.

ADE. They do.

NUGGET. Plant some seeds, sit in a deckchair, watch 'em grow. Maybe read some of those Greeks.

ADE. Men go to war, get dicked by the gods, come home.

NUGGET. You've ruined it now.

ADE. No, it's good – better than all that army-chick-lit.

NUGGET. I'll take your advice if you take mine. Go to uni, find a cushty job, fuck enough girls before you get married.

ADE. Spent my whole life in front of a screen, seen more war than soldiers in real war zones.

NUGGET. There's no wisdom there, son – anyone been through it'll tell you.

ADE. We need people to go to stop it happening – keep saying what it is till we get it into our skulls.

NUGGET. Afraid I can't help you, Adrian, but I enjoyed our little chat.

ADE. I've seen what it's going to be. Have to go, or it's all just theory – war-porn on the telly. I got to go do what you did – before it's too late.

NUGGET. You got to go do what I did?

ADE. Got to know what it is – risk my life to take another's.

NUGGET. Think maybe you got the wrong idea.

ADE. What do you mean?

NUGGET. Risked my own life enough times – never took another's.

ADE. You never killed no one?

NUGGET. Nothing to be proud of, never did what I was trained to do.

ADE. Why?

NUGGET. Came close enough times.

ADE. Were you afraid to do it?

NUGGET. Wouldn't call it fear. This old mullah and a boy come up to the checkpoint once, the old fella's waving his arms and the lad's grinning, but mad like, pushing a wheelbarrow. There's a body, young woman, kid's mum by all accounts, and she's had her foot blown off by a mine. Must've seen me coming, eh? I walk over to patch her up and just as I get there the boy pulls something… a string or something… and I see a bag of explosives under the woman… in the barrow. Well, something went wrong, coz it just sort of smoked and went all runny and the smell… poor woman had shat herself. Just then the old mullah pulls out a pistol, but I'm quick so we're just standing there. Know he's a knacker, know my SA80 is going to drop him, but I couldn't… his eyes, he was smiling, like the old bastard was ready for it, looking for it, his death, shining he was, like one of them paintings of Jesus, a Saint or something, and I just felt this… I felt this… joy… this is it… our destiny, the old man, the young boy, his mum… and the British soldier. I was two inches in tomorrow's newspaper… but it was beautiful. Apart from the unholy stench. Stood there like that… felt like fifteen years. The old boy coughed – something come up out of his lung, spat it on the floor, put his pistol in his pocket, said something to the boy, turned his wheelbarrow… and walked away. Can't explain that to this day.

ADE. A king used to lead his troops into battle. The Spartans, Romans, Alexander the Great – built civilisations on courage and honour. Their army was an inspiration to them.

NUGGET. Come in tomorrow, talk to Warrant Officer Jobson.

ADE. Do me now. Quickly. Get it over with.

NUGGET. Not on my last day.

ADE. I'm coming back, keep coming back till someone signs me.

NUGGET. Don't want to be watching out for you on the news.

ADE. I'll buy a ticket, fly there myself, be a mercenary, join them if I have to, don't care what side I'm on, I got to know what it is, before it's gone for ever.

NUGGET. I don't think it's going anywhere, Adrian. Come in tomorrow – they'll take you. They'll take you where you want to go.

2.7

FUTURE COMBAT SYSTEMS online.
New Clan Member Invitation.
Hi Ade…
Tom here…
U wanna pwn some n00bs?

A Nick Hern Book

First Person Shooter first published in Great Britain as a paperback original in 2010 by Nick Hern Books Limited, 14 Larden Road, London W3 7ST, in association with Birmingham Repertory Theatre

First Person Shooter copyright © 2010 Paul Jenkins

Paul Jenkins has asserted his right to be identified as the author of this work

Cover image: Indigo River
Cover design: Ned Hoste, 2H

Typeset by Nick Hern Books, London
Printed in Great Britain by CLE Print Ltd, St Ives, Cambs PE27 3LE

A CIP catalogue record for this book is available from the British Library

ISBN 978 1 84842 141 7